TURN

north

For additional resources or to order more books, visit:
www.GivingSquared.com/TurnNorth

Written by Joani Ross
With contributions from Emily Wilson, Senior, College of Charleston
© Giving Squared 2018

contents

Welcome	5
1. Freedom, Intentionality & Boundary Lines	9
2. But What About You? Who Do You Say I Am?	15
3. Always Remember Who You Are & Whose You Are	23
4. Exploring Your Calling	31
5. The Battlefield	39
6. Homesick & Finding A New Tribe	45
7. Speaking of Relationships...Let's Talk About Dating	51
8. Loving and Serving Others	57
9. Time Management & Time with God	61
10. Technology...For Better or Worse	67
11. Take Care of Yourself, Be Grateful & Enjoy the Journey	71
12. Rest & Reflection	77
Closing Thoughts & Resources	81
At-A-Glance Study Recap	83
TURN NORTH Bible Study	87
Journal Pages	139
Acknowledgements	150

"You've circled this mountain long enough, now **TURN NORTH**." Deuteronomy 2:3

welcome

"You've circled this mountain long enough, now **TURN NORTH**." (Deuteronomy 2:3)

This direction from God comes at the culmination of the Israelites wandering in the desert forty years. They are about to enter the promised land, a destination they have long desired to call home. However, while it is a beautiful place with lush landscapes, decadent fruit, and new adventures, the journey won't be easy. They are going into battle. The unknown, full of temptations from other cultures and plenty of false gods to worship surround them.

But God is on their side. He has ordained this place and time for them, and He stands ready to be with them every step of the way.

So as they pack up for this new leg of their life journey, God guides them saying, "now **TURN NORTH**."

Sweet sister, your time has come to enter this new territory God has also prepared for you. It can be scary, and it will be a battle, no doubt. But it is good. There are important things to experience and learn. Never forget that God is on your side.

Penned in this book are truths I want your heart to cling to, sprinkled with lessons-learned from girls a few years ahead of you, and a Bible study to complement each chapter. I want to equip you with tools to enter your new environment prepared and on a path leading to a purposeful and fulfilling college experience.

My prayer is that whatever direction your GPS takes you to your new college home, you will turn your heart, mind, and soul **NORTH**.

Eyes up and on Him. Facing God. Seeking God.

As a part of preparing for this study, in addition to much prayer and research, I surveyed over 325 girls from over 250 colleges and universities; girls from the large, secular universities to the small, intimate private Christian colleges, and everything in between. This book is written by me and all of these girls just a few years ahead of you. I can't wait to share the wisdom they have for you...things that caught them off guard as being so much harder than they thought, things they wish someone had told them, and advice from their personal experiences, triumphs, and mistakes.

People often say of college, "These are the best years of your life." When all you hear is how amazing college is, you create these expectations of what college life will look like...beautiful independence and freedom...instant besties who share your values, embrace your quirks from day one, and never let you down...Mr. Perfect grabbing a seat next to you in ENC class...sipping lattes on the lawn...one good time after another. You know, like all the social media pics you see of college life.

The following table shows the percentage of the college girls I surveyed who said it was extremely or somewhat hard when they first started college for each of the categories listed.

	All Schools	Secular Schools	Christian Schools	Community College
Academic pressures	84%	83%	86%	85%
Remembering my identity is in Christ (not other opinions, appearance, popularity, etc)	77%	77%	76%	73%
Finding a tribe/community that shares my values	68%	70%	51%	92%
Making new friends	64%	66%	56%	77%
Learning time management	64%	61%	68%	73%
Fitting in	57%	57%	57%	58%
Feeling homesick/lonely	55%	53%	68%	35%
Following God	53%	58%	44%	46%
Pressures around sex	34%	38%	26%	27%
Pressures around drinking	32%	36%	26%	23%

Percentage of survey respondents saying it was "extremely" or "somewhat" hard.

Girls, these are high percentages! Starting college isn't easy.

The college girls I surveyed wish they had known (and want you to know) these years, especially at the beginning, can be hard. It's not all glam and fun and carefree times with drama-free relationships. Many girls surveyed were caught off guard by the intense academic pressures, the difficulty in finding friends and community that shared their values, new levels of peer pressure, time management struggles, and homesickness they never anticipated.

None of this is to freak you out or squash your enthusiasm. Instead, it is to help you go in with eyes wide open and know YOU ARE NOT ALONE if you also find some of these areas difficult. Like all good things in life, it takes time, intentionality, and dedication to chart a new path, find your tribe, and get in your groove. Throughout this book I am going to help you navigate many of the areas those who have gone before you struggled with.

Each chapter contains the following:

- **Topical information** related to your new college journey.
- **ADVICE FROM YOUR OLDER SISTERS** section with wisdom and advice from girls in college and recent grads related to the topic.
- **LET'S CHAT** section containing discussion questions around the topic for you to consider and/or share with your small group.

The **BIBLE STUDY** in the back of your book contains twelve short Bible studies that correspond to each chapter's content. If you plan to do the Bible study along with the book, you can head over to that section after each chapter.

So, are you ready?

Grab your backpack,
your suitcase and favorite pillow,
your anticipation and trepidation,
and don't forget your Bible.

You've circled the mountain of this phase of your life long enough. **Let's head NORTH, girls**. Eyes up. Heart and mind open.

Oh, what a journey awaits you.

"The decisions you make determine the schedule you keep. The schedule you keep determines the life you live. And how you live your life determines how you spend your soul."
Lysa TerKeurst

"Begin as you mean to go on."
Charles Spurgeon

chapter 1

Freedom, Intentionality & Boundary Lines

"I was most caught off guard by the freedom of it all and having to adjust to being the one in charge of my life." University of Alabama, recent grad

As you will soon discover, college brings with it a floodgate of new freedoms. No one tells you where to be, when to be there, who to be there with, or what to do. Sounds amazing, right?

No doubt it can be amazing for sure. Until you cross lines you never meant to cross. Until you look back in several weeks, months, or even years with regret and say, "How did I get here? This isn't where I want to be."

There is a lot of pressure to fit in and be accepted in college. This kind of pressure is probably nothing new to you, but as you have likely discovered, fitting in at all costs and in the wrong ways does not translate to fulfillment and healthy relationships. Middle school and high school certainly provided a good training ground for this lesson. However, in college things get ramped up to a new level. Combine that with feeling a bit insecure about your new surroundings and being out of your safe comfort zone of home, and you can sometimes slip back into that approval pit...the go-along-to-get-along pit... that you may have mistakenly thought you had conquered.

Sweet sister, you don't have to have it all figured out (you won't!), but you do need to decide what values are non-negotiables and what you want your destination to look like. Without being intentional about the paths you take and anchored in the things that will get you where you want to be, the tides and currents of culture will have you drifting away...slowly, but steadily, sometimes without you even noticing until you are lost in dangerous waters, and no longer able see the shore.

Andy Stanley says, "We don't drift in good directions. We discipline and prioritize ourselves there." To do nothing is to drift.

College isn't a time to blindly go where the tides lead you and hope for the best. If you want to become the best version of you, intentionality matters. Sister, take control of your story starting now!

Think of college as a hands-on training ground to begin growing into the person you want to be...in friendships, career, leadership, relationships. College is a place to not only grow academically and in experience, but in true wisdom and character.

Use your new freedom well. Just because you can do something doesn't mean you should. Learn to practice discernment. Learn to say no when you know you should. Learn to take care of yourself. Learn to manage your time and to carve out space for God. Learn to turn north and seek God – not the world around you – for wisdom and direction. Learn to prioritize what is most important and live like the beloved child of God you are.

The college girls I surveyed want you to know that it was harder than they thought and the pressure is no joke. Have a vision for your destination, be aware of potential road hazards and distractions, and plan ahead about what boundary lines you want to draw. Boundary setting must be intentional because the cultural pull is always pressing against the line. It is so much easier to think through these things before you find yourself in a difficult position, vulnerable and teetering over the edge.

You might feel a little anxious now because you don't know your non-negotiables and you don't have a clear destination mapped out. That is okay! We will walk through many areas in the book to help you think through all of the pieces; to help you start identifying boundaries and things that truly matter to you; to start envisioning your destination and sketching out your path to get there.

Never forget that you have access to the greatest GPS, advocate, advisor, and friend who is with you always...the Holy Spirit; a direct line to God. Take advantage of it. Pray. Talk to Him. Ask Him to help you. He already knows the perfect path for you; the one He specifically created for you to walk down. He stands ready and willing to freely guide you.

advice
from your older sisters

"I wish I knew that everyone is experiencing what you are experiencing – it's not you alone." University of Florida, Freshman

"I wish I would have known how free I would be. It's a good thing and a bad thing. It's almost too free. I'm not forced to go to church, Bible study, or make the grades like I had been." Middle Tennessee State University, Junior

"Don't go into college thinking you are going to be able to fit in and make friends but also stand apart as a Christian without any effort. It is absolutely possible to do that, but you have to be intentional and realize that it's going to be hard to say no when you really want these people to like you." Carl Albert State College, Freshman

"I wish I knew that some people have a really, really, REALLY difficult transition to college & have a difficult time finding their people." Valdosta State University, Junior

"My advice would be to write a list of what you value before going to school and keep it in your planner. When you are checking out different organizations and deciding how you will spend your time during the first few weeks of college, keep that list nearby and ask yourself if you are upholding those values for yourself." Winona State University, Senior

"Set expectations for yourself before you're there, before you're in compromising situations. If you don't want to do something, make it clear to yourself and those you surround yourself with and hold to those standards. People will stop pressuring you for different things when they see you are serious." Cal State Monterey Bay, recent grad

"Peer pressure is a real thing. Especially for most people experiencing 'freedom' for the first time. It may feel like you need to try everything and get to know everyone. Instead focus on finding people who build you up. Focus on doing things that will strengthen your Walk with the Lord. Do not fall into the pressure." Southeastern University, recent grad

"I wish I didn't put so much pressure on myself for college to be the best 4 years of my life. Also knowing it's hard to meet people! I thought I would jump right in but it is definitely a process! I also was very prepared in saying no to drinking and going out and that was not as much of an issue as just meeting solid Christian friends." University of Georgia, Sophomore

"Going into college I was a very strong Christian, highly involved in church; I graduated from a private Christian high school. But none of that really prepared me for the pressures college had. Appearance, alcohol, and attention from boys were my down falls. I became the typical 'party girl' in a matter of DAYS. And before a full month could go by, I had given into A LOT of things I had always told myself I wouldn't do, or would wait for. The peer pressure and the desire to seem desirable was soooo overwhelming!" University of North Carolina at Charlotte, Sophomore

"I wish I knew that I wasn't alone, and there were other people on my school's campus who understood exactly what I was going though." Mars Hill University, Junior

"I wish someone told me it was going to be hard – like really hard. I would face things that challenged my everything, but that by surrendering, on my knees, face to the floor, to Jesus every day would get me through, and that it's always worth it in the end." Furman University, Senior

let's chat

What are your expectations for college life? What do you picture it being like?

What are you most excited about with regard to the freedom that college brings?

What are you most nervous about with regard to this newfound freedom?

What are your goals for college? Where do you see yourself in 5 years? 10 years? (if you don't know...that is OKAY, but take the time to think about it)

What will college have to look like to get there? What path will allow you to meet your goals? What can you do to make sure you draw appropriate boundary lines for the life you want to live in college before you have to face those challenges?

If you are doing the corresponding Bible study, head to page 91.

"It's not great faith you need.
It's faith in a great God."
NT Wright

"What comes to mind
when we think about God
is the most important
thing about us."
A.W. Tozer

chapter 2

But what about you? Who do YOU say that I am?

Who do you say God is? How you answer this question shapes your worldview, which shapes the subsequent decisions you make in all areas of your life. Without a solid view of who God is you won't put much stock in who He says you are or what path He says you should be on.

There is a difference in knowing about God (facts about Him, or simply believing He exists) and trusting and believing IN Him (the fullness of who He is, and putting your faith in Him as your Lord and Savior). The Bible tells us that even the devil believes in God, but he has chosen to oppose God rather than follow Him and submit to Him. Powered by pride and self-absorption, the devil choses to go at life following his own rules, seeking to create his own empire and please his own desires. He is crafty in trying to pull us into his destructive way of thinking and living.

You can only go through the motions for so long over something you don't genuinely believe. Without a firm footing, you will fall away easily when challenged...and college is full of attempts to challenge your beliefs.

So, before you go any further, it is important to really think about your view of God and His place in your life and decision making. Where your faith up until this point may have been largely influenced by others, college is a time – if you haven't already – to make your faith YOUR OWN; to make God personal to you.

Your relationship with God impacts your genuine response to Him. Too often we limit our focus to the response side -- trying to be good, going to church, trying to obey His commands, going to youth group, reading the Bible, etc. – rather than grounding ourselves in WHO GOD IS to us personally.

Don't get me wrong, the response matters for sure. But what is your why? Why do you do these things? Is it because you don't want to disappoint your family? Is it because you are afraid of hell? Is it because that is just what people tell you to do? Or, is it because you really love God and believe HIs ways are the best ways?

Your why matters. It is far more valuable to focus on WHO GOD IS than what you can or should be doing for Him...because once your view of God is right, the rest will naturally follow. It doesn't mean you know and understand everything. No one does, or will, on this side of Heaven. God is far too big for our simple understanding. But it does mean you believe IN HIM, and you believe HIM. When you genuinely believe He is in control of all things, He loves you, He has your best interest in mind, He is on the winning side, then you will naturally and willfully choose HIM to be your counselor and guide rather than the pulls of your surroundings.

Do you have a BIG view of God...that He is powerful, holy, good, in control, able, mighty, consistent, righteous, merciful, loving?

Do you believe He is who He says? That He keeps His promises? That He can do what He says He will do? Do you believe God created you and has good plans in store for you?

Do you believe that God is big enough to guide you, handle your burdens, forgive your sins, give you peace, have your good in mind, care about what happens to you? WHATEVER is going on in your life, God is big enough- do you believe this?

During these college years, as you are soaking in knowledge, commit to learning also about God. Study His Word and promises. Get to know Him personally. Proactively make efforts to put yourself in places where you can see and experience His glory and power. He is always available to you... in your dorm, your classroom, your walk, your shower, your bed... everywhere! As one of the college girls I surveyed says, "Chase after God!"

On the next two pages are some Scripture references about who God is. Take time to read these and reflect on His character. Ask Him to give you wisdom and understanding. He wants nothing more than for you to personally KNOW HIM.

God is love … He is the definition and example of love - 1 John 4:8

God is not limited … He is for all generations, for all time - Psalm 33:11

God sees everything … nothing is missed by Him- Psalm 33:13

God is preparing a place for you to dwell with Him-Revelation 21:3

God is in control of everything- Job 12:10

God is a creator … all things were created by Him- Genesis 1:1

God is merciful, gracious, loving, faithful, steadfast- Exodus 34:6

God is with you, fighting for you- Deuteronomy 20:4

God is near to you when you draw near to Him- James 4:8

God will never leave, destroy, or forget you- Deuteronomy 4:31

God is not partial … he is great, mighty, and full of justice-Deuteronomy 10:17-18

God is the light … His way is perfect … His Word is true-2 Samuel 22:29-31

God keeps His Word … He doesn't lie or change His mind- Numbers 23:19

God is gracious & merciful … He waits for you to come to Him- 2 Chronicles 30:9

God is faithful … providing a way to escape temptation-1 Corinthians 10:13

God is light … in Him there is no darkness-1 John 1:5

God is patient … wishing all reach repentance- 2 Peter 3:9

God is living & active -Hebrews 4:12

God is ruler over all ... more powerful than anyone- Isaiah 40:23

God gives good gifts ... everything thing good comes from God- James 1:17a

God is consistent ... in Him there is no variation or change - James 1:17b

God loves you ... enough to send His son to die-John 3:16

God is a provider ... He provides for all His creation- Matthew 6:26

God is perfect ... His Word is true; He is your shield - Psalm 18:30

God is a righteous judge - Psalm 50:6

God has always been here & will always be here-Psalm 90:2

God is gracious, righteous, & merciful- Psalm 116:5

God gives you the free gift of eternal life- Romans 6:23

God bears your burdens ... He is your salvation- Psalm 68:19

God bestows favor & honor ... He withholds nothing good-Psalm 84:11

God is everywhere ... He knows and sees all-Psalm 139:7

God is with you wherever you go- Joshua 1:9

God forgives ... He does not retain His anger- Micah 7:18

God is your rock...He is a refuge and He will steady you-2 Samuel 22:32-34

God knows everything- 1 John 3:20

God gives wisdom- James 1:5

Visit www.givingsquared.com/TurnNorth for a printable of the GOD IS passages that includes the referenced Scripture.

advice
from your older sisters

"Understand the reasons you believe what you do. I was told I would face certain things (alcohol, boys, peer pressure…), but what I realized was when I did stand up and say no, people wanted to know why, and I had to give them an answer. Not only for them, but for myself. Know your why." Furman University, Senior

"I wish I knew how to study the Bible and how to have a relationship with God. Even though I grew up in church and knew a lot of the Bible, I didn't have that DEEP relationship." Cal State Fullerton, Junior

"I wish I had been stronger in my faith and less likely to conform to the world." Baylor University, Junior

"I wish I knew I wasn't as strong of a Christian as I thought." Liberty University, recent grad

"I wish I would have known that no matter how strong you think you are in Christ, and even if you really are strong in Him, It's HARD! It's hard to deliberately not fit in and do what everyone else is doing. I wish someone would have told me I wasn't as strong and holy as I thought I was because it really tests you and your faithfulness." Carl Albert State College, Freshman

"Time management is everything. SO many people around you feel just as lost and scared about the unknown as you do. There is absolutely no pressure to find the perfect career or 'soulmate'…God has perfect plans. Trying to figure out life without a strong, intentional, personal relationship with God is like trying to sled without the snow…there's no point." Calvin College, Sophomore

"Build your foundation on Christ, so when you think the world is falling apart you can fall on God." Vanguard, Sophomore

"Always take time for God! Especially in college!" Black Hills State University, Freshman

"It's going to be hard and you will probably face the biggest reshaping of your faith throughout college as you learn and are given new perspectives. The most important thing to remember is who you are and whose you are because God loves you no matter the circumstances." Palm Beach Atlantic University, Senior

"Remember that God loves you and sees that you're trying!! You don't need to do ANYTHING for Him to love you." Michigan State University, Senior

let's chat

On a scale of 1-10, how strong would you say your belief and faith in God are? It's okay to be honest here. Getting to know God is a life-long endeavor.

Why do you think your belief in God is so foundational for everything else in your life?

Take a look at the "God is" passages on the previous pages (and with the actual Scripture cited on www.givingsquared.com/TurnNorth). Which ones stand out to you most?

How would you describe God to someone who didn't know Him? Practice putting into words who God is to you. If you are reading this book with friends, take turns sharing your responses. If you are doing this study on your own, practice your response out loud.

If you are doing the corresponding Bible study, head to page 95.

You are enough.
You are so enough.
It is so unbelievable
how enough you are.

Jesus looks at the cross
and then looks at you
and says, "she's worth it!"
Every. Single. Time.
Every. Single. Day.
Never forget.

chapter 3

Always Remember WHO You Are and WHOSE You Are

I've always thought a girl heading to college should be able to bring her loyal, trusted dog with her. I picture a rectangular dorm layout with rooms around the outside and a huge courtyard/dog park in the middle. Our dogs always think we are amazing just the way we are. We are absolute perfection in their eyes. When I walk in the door – no matter how long or short I have been gone – my dog greets me with exuberant joy. He jumps up and down, wags his tail, and begs for my full attention. I've gotten in the habit of saying to him, "Chester, I see you, and I love you."

And I think this is what God is always saying to us. "[insert your name], I SEE you, and I LOVE you." On your best days and your worst days, God sees you. He knows what you are going through. He knows what you have done and what has been done to you. And He loves you so much. Every. Single. Time. He can't wait for you to come to Him. THIS is who you are.

In college, a new world is opening up to you, and it may be a bit of a culture shock with so many new outside forces trying to lay claim to who you are.

Don't let other people, your circumstances, your stress level, your grades, your professors, your social life, or your social media feed tell you who you are. Only God gets to do this.

My pastor, Joby Martin, reminds us over and over, "You are not your sin, your past, your addiction or your mistakes...."

I'll add...you are not your friend group, your sorority, your major, your GPA, your social status, your appearance, your jean size, your attendance at parties, your achievements, your bank account, your last drink, your boyfriend, your social media followers.

Joby continues, "...Jesus is the only one who gets to tell you who you are. And He says you are righteous and redeemed."

Too often we tell ourselves, "if I could only get into that college...date that guy...pledge that sorority...break into that friend group...win that award...get those grades...land that leadership role...pull myself together...make that team, etc., THEN I would be part of something special. THEN I would BE something special." Our identity gets wrapped in our activities, accomplishments, and associations. While these things can be amazing, they will never fully satisfy us. They will always be lacking.

Just as your mistakes, sins, and failures don't define you, neither do your activities, awards or achievements. God alone is the source of your identity. Nothing you do or don't do will change that.

Sweet sister, your identity is in Christ. This is an unwavering truth amidst the highs and lows of life (and there will be many!). God's opinion is the only one you can count on; the only one that never changes.

When you feel those tinges of unworthiness, shame, comparison (or on the flipside, pride or condemnation of others), this is a signal that you are rooting your identity in things other than God's truths. Take a timeout to remind yourself of your true identity from the giver of all good things...

> You are a child of God! You are created in His image and likeness!
> You are forgiven and free! You are an heir to the kingdom of God!
> You are beautiful! You are valuable!
> You have a purpose and calling that will bring Him glory!
> You have HUGE things to step into created just for you!

You are so very loved...exactly how you are right now...not the future, cleaned up, or improved version of you, but the YOU RIGHT NOW!

On the next two pages are Scripture references about who God says you are. If you are struggling with your identity, take the time to read over these verses and fill your mind with Truth about who you are. Commit to reading them nightly before bed or first thing in the morning. If there are some that are really resonating with you, type them into your phone notes or make a wallpaper photo out of them to save on your phone as a reminder. You are who GOD SAYS you are, sweet sister!

God says you are...

You are created in the image and likeness of God. (Genesis 1:27)

You are fearfully and wonderfully made. (Psalm 139:14)

You are more than a conqueror. (Romans 8:37)

You are no longer a slave to sin. (Romans 6:6)

You are a child of God. (John 1:12 and 1 John 3:1)

You are not condemned. (Romans 8:1)

You can never be separated from God's love. (Romans 8:38-39)

You are chosen to bear fruit that lasts. (John 15:16)

You, with other believers, form one body. (Romans 12:5)

You are one with Christ. (1 Corinthians 6:17)

You are chosen, holy, royal; a special possession of God. (1 Peter 2:9)

You have wisdom from God. (1 Corinthians 1:30)

Your labor is not in vain. (1 Corinthians 15:58)

You are a new creation. (2 Corinthians 5:17)

You are a friend of God. (John 15:15)

You are an adopted child of God. (Ephesians 1:5)

You are God's child. (Galatians 3:26)

You have every spiritual blessing, (Ephesians 1:3)

You are redeemed and forgiven of all of your sins. (Ephesians 1:7)

You are clothed and one in Christ. (Galatians 3:27-28)

You have Christ living in you. (Galatians 2:20)

You are chosen. (Ephesians 1:11)

You are for the praise of his glory. (Ephesians 1:12)

You have been seated in the heavenly realms. (Ephesians 2:6)

You've been given the incomparable riches of God's grace. (Ephesians 2:7)

You are God's handiwork; you are created for good works. (Ephesians 2:10)

You, who were once far away, have been brought near. (Ephesians 2:13)

You are built together as a holy building. (Ephesians 2:22)

You are a Temple. (1 Corinthians 6:19-20)

You may approach God with freedom and confidence. (Ephesians 3:12)

You are light. (Ephesians 5:8)

Your citizenship is in Heaven. (Philippians 3:20)

You have been given power, love, and self-control. (2 Timothy 1:7)

Your joy overflows. (Philippians 1:26)

All your needs are met according to his glorious riches. (Philippians 4:19)

You are holy and faithful. (Colossians 1:2)

You are held together in Him. (Colossians 1:17)

You have hope of glory. (Colossians 1:27)

You will become fully mature. (Colossians 1:28)

You have hidden treasures of wisdom and knowledge. (Colossians 2:3)

You are rooted and built up. (Colossians 2:7)

You have been given the fullness of the deity. (Colossians 2:9-10)

You are raised with Christ. (Colossians 3:1-4)

You will rise from the dead. (1 Thessalonians 4:16)

You can give thanks in all circumstances. (1 Thessalonians 5:18)

You have faith, hope, and love. (1Timothy 1:14)

Visit www.givingsquared.com/TurnNorth for a printable of the GOD SAYS YOU ARE passages that includes the referenced Scripture.

advice
from your older sisters

"I wish coming into college I had a stronger identity in Christ and not worldly things." Ole Miss, Freshman

"I wish I had known that nothing besides Christ will ever satisfy my desire to have an 'identity'. That in him I am loved, preferred, understood and desired in a way I never will be by anyone else…even by my best friends and future husband. I am still learning this but didn't have the first clue in college and it was the blind leading the blind! Also, I wish I had a better grasp on the Word and how dynamic, alive, and encouraging it is." University of Alabama, recent grad

"I wish I had believed more genuinely in God's love for me and believed what the Bible said about me over the lies of the world." University of Georgia, Senior

"Before you go and try to find yourself in the world, know who you are in God's eyes. It makes all the difference. You are worthy and valuable. Once you know this, your standards are set high and you can face the challenges ahead with grace and strength in the Lord!" Colorado Christian University, Sophomore

"Always remember: you are worthy, you are enough, and you are loved." Lancaster Bible College, Sophomore

"Always remember who you are but most importantly, WHOSE you are. You are a daughter of the King so act like it. Don't get caught up in the drama and no matter how busy and frustrated you may get, always be kind and maintain your relationship with Christ." Valdosta State University, Sophomore

"Your identity is not in your test grades. Your identity is not in which sorority you are part of. Your identity is not in your major. Your identity is not in what mistakes you have made. Your identity is in Christ. You are made new in him. You are a child of God." Southcentral Kentucky Community College, Sophomore

"Girl, you are stronger than all those struggles you will face. The devil may be whispering in your ear, but always remember your God is in your soul fighting for you." East Tennessee State University, recent grad

"Remember that feelings (like...I don't have real friends, my friends don't like me, guys don't like me, I'll never get engaged, etc.) are not facts and do not actually dictate your worth or identity. These feelings are fleeting but the presence of God is permanent and can be experienced at any time, but it takes commitment to realize the ways he pursues you and to build a relationship with him. Be intentional about the time you spend with God and with other people." University of Alabama, recent grad

"Just remember that your identity is found in Jesus and only Jesus. He's the only one that can fill any feeling of loneliness even in the toughest times. Be yourself and make friends! Don't be afraid to let your personality and love for Jesus shine! Soon you'll come to find that you're not so alone in your pursuit of Him after all. Don't feel pressured to do what everyone else is doing. If it doesn't feel right or seem right, don't do it and don't worry about being judged over it." UNLV, grad student

"Run so fast after God and His approval that nothing else matters. Your GPA doesn't define you, your friends don't define you, your boyfriend/husband doesn't define you, your past doesn't define you. All of these definitions pale in comparison to who God says you are." Moody Bible Institute, grad student

let's chat

If you had to describe yourself to someone, what words would you use?

Where do you generally go to define your identity?

What makes it hard to believe what God says about who you are?

Who do you say God says you are?

Take a look at the **GOD SAYS YOU ARE** passages on the previous pages (and with the actual Scripture cited on www.givingsquared.com/TurnNorth). Which ones stand out to you most? Which provide you with the most comfort?

If you are doing the corresponding Bible study, head to page 99.

"I used to be afraid of failing
at something that really mattered to me,
but now I'm more afraid of succeeding
at things that don't matter."
Bob Goff

chapter 4

Exploring Your Calling

I'm guessing a question you have been asked – or will be asked – a million times is, "what are you majoring in?" or "what do you want to do with your life?"

Some people enter this new phase of life with a crystal-clear vision of where they want to go and how they plan to get there. Others don't have a clue. Wherever you find yourself on this spectrum, keep an open mind and an open line of communication with God.

College is unique season of life to explore and learn. It is a time to dig into who you are, what you want to do, and how God fits into all of it. Take advantage of the vast resources and opportunities available to you as a student.

Know that God has created you with unique callings. He has set apart good works for you to step in to. There are things that only you can accomplish with your specific giftings, experiences, and personality type.

While your overarching mission is to glorify God and make disciples, within that, you were created with beautiful purpose. Take the time to explore your passion and purpose. Pray about your calling as you sign up for new classes, join different groups, meet new people, and research volunteer and leadership opportunities.

Don't look to the left or right in comparison of other girls' callings. TURN NORTH. Look up. Look for God to show you and guide you. I believe we are most in sync with God and how He created us – and the peace, joy, and satisfaction that comes from that – when we are living out our unique and personal calling. Other girls' callings don't quite fit us right.

Don't hide behind others either, being afraid to do what God called you to, thinking you don't have the skills or experience or resources or presence. One of my favorite quotes is, "God doesn't call the equipped; He equips the called." You will never feel 100% ready. Often you just have to go scared and trust where God is leading you. He wants you to rely on Him!

Don't be afraid to try new things and don't ever be afraid to fail. Failure is part of the journey and is an excellent teacher. The most successful people often cite specific failures as pivotal moments in their story.

Some of the college girls I surveyed mentioned how devastated they or their friends were over certain closed doors, whether college admissions, sorority recruitment, leadership opportunities, etc. Sister, hear this... Sometimes God closes doors because He knows you won't, and He knows what is best for you. As painful as it feels at the time, His vision far exceeds ours and we don't always want what is best for us long term. We can't yet see the full picture as He does. Rachel Hollis says, "God has perfect timing, and it's highly possible that by not being where you thought you should be, you will end up exactly where you are meant to go."

Even the most unlikely roads can be used to shape you, teach you, stretch you and even introduce you to new things you never considered or realized you loved and were good at.

Let God be your guide and then pray for boldness to step into the things He tells you to. Pray for endurance to stay on the path He shows you and to not be distracted by the flashy signs, roadblocks, and detours of the world designed to get you off track. Faithfully trust God's prompting when another path might be best.

As part of the LET'S CHAT section, I've included several prompts to think about directions you might want to explore. They are also available in printable form at www.givingsquared.com/TurnNorth . You can add to them over time and refer to them when you are considering your major, electives to take, volunteer or leadership activities to explore, etc. Spend time in prayer asking God to show you paths to walk down and doors to walk through.

advice
from your older sisters

"I wish I had known that the whole future doesn't have to be planned out your first semester of college. Take time to really know yourself and focusing on following God's true plan for your life." Southeastern University, recent grad

"I wish I had chosen a major based on God's plan and what His plan is for me." The University of Alabama at Birmingham, Junior

"I would say not to worry too much about the future and what you will do with your life. It's also completely normal to change your major several times and be super confused. People think you have to know what you want to do before you go to college or you will just fall way behind, but that's not all true. Just trust that God will guide you in the career path you will need to take. Jeremiah 29:11" East Tennessee State University, Junior

"Don't be afraid of failure. Sometimes being knocked down is for the best, but as long as you keep your eyes on the prize then you can do anything. Don't be afraid to change your major if you find out it's not for you." Bellarmine University, Sophomore

"You are in college to do your own thing that God has called you to do. You are called to serve the Lord's purpose for you; you are called to spread the joy, love, peace, patience, kindness, and compassion of Jesus. Don't forget who you find your identity in." Texas State University, Sophomore

"Be who God created you to be. If you don't know who you are, find rest in knowing that God has a divine purpose for your life. You are here for a reason. You are important." Dallas Baptist University, Senior

"You don't have to be perfect and have your whole future figured out. God has a higher plan that we won't be able to figure out. Have balance in all aspects of your life. Learn how to glorify God in all things." University of Virginia, Senior

"There may be times when you feel that you might have made a wrong decision – about what school you're at, what major you choose, or any of the other numerous decisions you're facing currently. Just know that even at times when you're not comfortable or certain, you can still be right where Jesus needs you to be. Change is hard to prepare for, no matter how excited we may be for it. Your strength is limited, but Christ's is an endless well from which you can draw from. If you're feeling confused, frightened, or alone, turn to Him. He is your Father, and He longs to make you feel whole and loved. Trust His heart, even when you can't trace His hand." John Brown University, Junior

"Find out what you're passionate about. It could be service, it could be evangelism, or something else. When you find what you are passionate about, it can give you a good idea of God's purpose for your life. He can use your passions to better His kingdom." The University of Alabama, Junior

let's chat

So, what's your major 😊 ? What are you thinking you want to pursue career-wise?

Flip through the CALLING prompts on the following pages (printable worksheets also available at www.givingsquared.com/TurnNorth) and begin working through some of the questions. Which are easier to fill out? Which are harder?

Brainstorm three things you can do this year to discover and/or grow in your calling space:

1.

2.

3.

If you are doing the corresponding Bible study, head to page 103.

your passion

What do you love?

What makes you happy?

What gets your heart beating with excitement?

What types of things do you tend to gravitate toward?

If you could have or do anything, what would it be?

What things do you look at someone else and say, I wish I could do that? (not to compare/copy, but to see where your passions are stirred toward something...you will find your unique spin on it)

What do you dream about doing?

What did you dream about doing when you were a kid?

What would you do if time and money were no obstacle?

What do you spend your spare time on or can't wait to do?

What inspires you? What about it inspires you?

Who inspires you? What about them inspires you?

What gives you energy or fires you up when you are doing it?

What type of content do you reach for when you want to learn about something?

If someone told you to search the web for one hour, what would you start searching for?

What do you want to be remembered for when people look back on your life?

gifts + experiences

What are you naturally good at?

What do you get complimented on?

What kinds of experience do you have?

What tough things have you gone through in your life?

What do others say you're are good at?

Where do you do something and feel a great accomplishment?

What are unique experiences you have gone through?

What things do your friends/family/community turn to you to help with?

What are your personality type and spiritual gifts? (links to assessments are in the downloadable calling tab at www.givingsquared.com/TurnNorth)

needs

Where do you see a need that isn't being met? (family, friends, community, the world)

What kinds of needs do you want to meet?

What kinds of things do you hear about and feel outraged or your heart breaks?

Where do you want to see a change in your community? In the world?

What fears do you have for those coming up behind you?

girlfriend chat

Often other people can see things in you that you can't see in yourself. Grab a trusted friend or two and ask them what they see as your passion and gifting.

What do you think I am good at?

When have you seen me light up the most?

What unique skills have you seen me display?

What kinds of things do you see me easily gravitate toward?

Where do you see people coming to me for advice?

brainstorm

Take a look at all of your lists and write down some options that seem to cover these areas. Keep an open mind…don't be shy. Just because it is on paper doesn't mean you have to do it. This is a space to explore and generate ideas. Often one idea leads to another until you uncover gold.

_____
_____
_____
_____
_____
_____
_____

chapter 5

The Battlefield

You are on a path to fulfill your calling, and that ticks the devil off.

Your college campus is a wonderful, exciting place...but it is also likely to present one of the fiercest battlefields you have stepped foot on in your life to date. It is critical to prepare for what is to come...an intense battle for your heart, mind, and soul. I say this not to scare you, but to tell you to get battle-ready, girl!

A favorite quote of mine says, "The enemy is not fighting you because you are weak, he's fighting you because you have purpose." When you are strong and confident in the power of God and your identity in Him, the devil knows he doesn't stand a chance. He will do anything to cause wedges of doubt, and he will use people and circumstances as weapons.

Pressures from all sides to party, drink, have sex, maintain stellar grades, get uber involved, forge bridesmaid-worthy friendships, live in unity with a difficult roommate you didn't choose, and more surround you...but always remember, the real enemy is not these decisions or pressures or people. The heart of the matter is the condition of your heart. The enemy is sin and Satan, and he is after your heart and mind.

Paul tells us of the battle, "For we do not wrestle against flesh and blood, but against the rulers, against the authorities, against the cosmic powers over this present darkness, against the spiritual forces of evil in the heavenly places." (Ephesians 6:12)

In other words, the battle goes deeper and higher than you think. Your greatest enemy is not the person to the left or right. It's not your professor or roommate. It's not that girl who left you out or that guy who left you heartbroken. It's not the people who taunt you or the people who tempt you. It's not people who look different or think different. It is the devil. HE IS THE ENEMY.

He is waging war in places unseen using his weapons of lies, manipulation, oppression, pressure, comparison, critique, differences, strong opinions, entitlement, unforgiveness. He has chosen college campuses as one of his favorite battlefields. Don't waste your fight on flesh and blood. You'll be fighting the wrong fight.

Spiritual forces of evil. A masterful enemy, Satan. What's a girl to do?

Paul's advice to you and me in the battlefield has two parts:

1. Be STRONG IN THE LORD and in the strength of HIS MIGHT. Do you feel a little weak? A little out-matched? No worries! We don't have to be strong in our own abilities. The strength of the Lord is where it's at.
2. Put on the FULL ARMOR OF GOD. Some won't do. A piece here and there won't cut it in this fierce battle. We need the WHOLE armor of God.

It is an ongoing process of trusting God and staying connected to His power, then getting up and doing it again. Daily reapplying His armor.

Oswald Chambers says, "It is easy for us to imagine that we will suddenly come to a point in our lives where we are fully prepared, but preparation is not suddenly accomplished. The Christian life requires preparation and more preparation."

The devil wants nothing more than to get your eyes off of Jesus and your feet off of His path for you. When you feel that battle raging around you, call out the name of JESUS. His name has power. Remember you are fighting in God's strength. If you are on His side, He is on your side. This battle, though tough at times, will make you stronger in the end. Through it, you will build not only your academic and experience resume but also grow in character and faith. You will gain confidence that in Him you can overcome and do hard things.

Character bloomed from God's strength experienced in the battles of life, and planted in His promises, is what will make you successful.

Suit up, sister!

advice
from your older sisters

"I wish I had known how much college is set up against the average Christian ideology set and values." Fitchburg State University, Sophomore

"Young people starting college can easily be brainwashed from what we've learned growing up. The enemy works through the system to make us forget the only truth – JESUS is the way to EVERYTHING. And there's nothing this world needs more right now than Him. So, stay ROOTED in the foundation that's been laid on you! Guard your heart above all else. Remember that He is with you." Valencia College, Freshman

"Colleges preach diversity and inclusion but that really only happens if you follow the mainstream or leftist lifestyle. Coming from a conservative Christian household I wasn't accepted for who I was on campus and was openly scorned for my character." University of Michigan, Sophomore

"I was caught off guard by the amount of temptations when it comes to drinking and parties." University of South Florida, Freshman

"Pray that God sends you the right friends. If you surround yourself with God-fearing people, the pressures of sex and drinking are not so hard." Colorado State University-Pueblo, graduate student

"Just because you THINK everyone is doing something doesn't really mean everyone is doing it. Find people that share your same values and won't pressure you into thinking otherwise." Iowa State University, Sophomore

"I was caught off guard at the realization that I have extremely different values and morals compared to so many on campus." Red Deer College, Junior

"It's hard! It is so easy to fall off the wagon and into temptation. Find your identity in Christ. When you center yourself in Christ, everything else will fall into place." Middle Tennessee State University, Junior

"Please stay close to God. It's hard. It's so hard, but it is so worth it. I walked away for a while and it was the worst time of my life. My Pastor said something during service one day about how our worst day with God is still better than our best day without him. I can't explain how true that is, but please don't get to the point where you learn how true that is. Trust that he's got you the whole time and stay true to him even when it gets hard." East Stroudsburg University, Senior

"Don't feel like you're missing out when it seems EVERYONE you know is hitting the frat parties and you're studying at home. Try to find a godly friend group that you can still have fun with without making choices you'll regret later." Baylor University, Junior

"Memorize helpful verses from the Bible because having them in the back of your mind will be the most beneficial thing you can do for yourself when you are going through trials." Cal Lutheran, Sophomore

"On days when it seems hardest, turn to God in prayer. You may not understand everything that is going on at first, but someday when you look back on your college years, you will understand how going through these trials formed you into who you will be." Christendom College, recent grad

Emily Wilson, a Senior at the College of Charleston, shares this advice she received her freshman year, "The devil is going to make it as uncomfortable as he possibly can for you to proclaim your faith on your campus because he's hoping you'll just give up on it when it gets too awkward." She continues with this advice, "God is the only being in the universe who is omniscient. That means that Satan can't hear your personal thoughts and silent prayers. Sometimes, you need to just get on your knees and pray out loud for God to fill up the space you're in and command Satan to get away from you. Demons will flee at the mention of the name of Jesus, but only if they can hear it."

let's chat

What kind of warfare do you think you will face in college? Look back at the survey results in the introduction (pg. 6). Are you surprised by how hard the college girls surveyed found some of these things? What pieces of "armor" will be helpful with each?

How can knowing you are stepping into a battlefield help you recognize the enemy's schemes when they come, and to stand strong against them?

How can you look at a battle and see Satan's work in it? How can he twist things to make us focus on other people and circumstances instead of recognizing that it is him at work?

What can you do to get – and stay – battle ready?

If you are doing the corresponding Bible study, head to page 107.

"One of the primary tools of the enemy is isolation."
Joby Martin

How many of the people I surround myself with care about the condition of my soul?

chapter 6

Homesick & Finding a New Tribe

"There are people out there like you!! You just have to find them." Boston College, Junior

Gone are the days where everything is familiar and comfortable, where you could always find family or friends nearby. Though you dreamed of this day, you are suddenly displaced. It doesn't quite feel like home yet. So. Many. New. People. So many new places. It is simultaneously exciting and frightening.

Whether you are terrified to move to your new city and school, or if you are dying to get the heck out of town and start college, you will experience times feeling homesick. You will miss the familiar comfort of home. Please know that you are not alone. Everyone – even those who seem the most outgoing and plugged in – have moments of feeling homesick. It is completely normal (and temporary) in this new phase of your life.

New places invite the scary task of finding a new tribe. It isn't easy, sweet sister. In fact, it can feel so hard at times, you might decide you are better off on your own…you'll just keep your head in your books. But community matters a lot. The essence of God is community as God is three persons – the Father, Son, and Holy Spirit. We were created in God's image and likeness. We were made for community. We need each other! Don't cling so tightly to the past and your hometown that you can't make room to appreciate and flourish in your new home.

As you seek out new community, make sure it reflects your values. Motivational speaker Jim Rohn says, "You are the average of the five people you spend the most time with." True or not, the point is valid that the people you hang out with rub off on you. You pick up their habits and mannerisms, and even their values.

Seek out a Godly tribe where you lift each other up, never tear each other down. A group that shares your values, is safe to explore these new life changes, and hold each other accountable. Some things you join will provide a wide range of acquaintances, and that is okay. But also look for those places where you can build deep and healthy friendships. Even one or two close relationships will positively impact your college experience.

Find a tribe that will chill with you when you have had a crazy day, run the stadiums with you when you need to blow off some energy, pray with you when you are facing a tough decision, bring over a pint of ice cream when your heart is broken, prayerfully process these crazy life changes with you. Friends who will gently and lovingly call you out when you are veering off track. Friends who encourage you to be who God created you to be. And you need to be this friend too. There is nothing more special than beautiful friendship.

So, how do you find your tribe? One of the most commonly cited pieces of advice from my survey of over 300 college girls was to get plugged in EARLY. Even if it means trying a few different student ministries, school sponsored organizations, churches, or groups to find one you feel at home in…do it! Keep trying. Building community and establishing genuine friendships takes time and effort, but it is so worth it!

A hard truth in all life stages is that friends will sometimes disappoint you. We are all flawed and a work in progress. Envy, fear, selfishness, and pride get in the way and splinter or even destroy friendships. Always remember that God is faithful even when friends are not. Be quick to not make assumptions, to give the benefit of the doubt, to show grace, and forgive easily. But know when to walk away from a toxic friendship.

As hard as it is, it is important to put yourself out there. It may take a while, but stick with it. Break through the awkwardness and say hello. Participate in that activity. Try out that new club. Don't wait for friendships to come to you; take the initiative to find your community. Trust me, with very few exceptions, everyone is craving community and just as nervous about the newness of it all as you are!

Your tribe is out there, sweet sister. Before you know it, you will look back on this season of your life and be so grateful you took the time to find your people.

advice
from your older sisters

"I expected to be homesick but I didn't expect it to be something I battled every day. As a sophomore, I am much better, but homesickness was my biggest struggle my freshmen year." Mississippi State University, Sophomore

"I wish that I had joined a small group earlier in my college career. That has been one of the most valuable tools for me over the past 6 months of college."

"Just know that everything you are feeling is valid. You're going through a huge life change and everyone adjusts in their own way and in their own time. There's absolutely no shame in feeling homesick, calling your mom every day, or going home every other weekend. Just make it a priority to find a church home-away-from-home and plug into a small group or other ministry. Fellowship and community are vital for a relationship with God and, in my case, for my mental health. As badly as you may want to stay cooped up in your dorm room, get involved and take advantage of every opportunity to build the Kingdom." College of Charleston, Senior

"I wish I knew that there were other people seeking a community of people who were strong in their faith like I was. I felt alone because I didn't know anyone else who prayed or read their bible." Illinois State University, Sophomore

"You become who you hang around. If you have around parties, that's what you'll do. If you hand around people growing in their faith, that's what you'll do. It's up to you to decide how you want to be influenced and by who." Wayne State College, recent grad

"Find people who help you find God." Marian University, Freshman

"Love yourself enough to walk away from people who do not respect you." Dyersburg State Community College, Freshman

"I wish I had taken the time to scope out possible churches in the area and done research to see what Christian orgs were on campus." Mount Holyoke College, Junior

"I wish someone had told me that you are probably not going to meet all of your very best friends the first week of school. Good things take time and it's okay to not have a thousand friends. Just get plugged in and put yourself in an environment where you will be surrounded by likeminded people. The Lord will handle the rest! You will find your heart people in time." Liberty University, Sophomore

"Be open to new people and new experiences! If you get homesick (I did), put yourself out there and do things instead of wallowing in your dorm alone." Hope College, recent grad

"It's so important to make friends and have a support group, but just make sure you're making the right friends." Campbell University, Sophomore

"When I look back, my biggest regret was not putting myself out there. It is so easy to find comfort in doing your own thing, but never really putting yourself out of your comport zone. It was only when I stepped out of my comfort zones that I saw fruit. I forced myself to go to a new church by myself when I didn't know anyone. I have never experienced Christian community or more diligent teaching than I have at the church I now call home." University of Alabama at Birmingham, recent grad

"Know that you are not the only one that is lonely and trying to find friends with the same values. Finding those friends may take a few months or even an entire semester, but don't get discouraged. There's going to be pressures to drink or do drugs because it's the 'normal' thing to do in college, but know there are other people out there not looking to get involved in those activities." Texas A&M, grad student

"When you surround yourself with friends who share your faith, it will be easier to work together for God's kingdom while avoiding the social pressures associated with college (drinking, sex, etc.)" Appalachian State University, grad student

"I would give a friend the advice to really put yourself out there the first couple weeks of school. It will be very hard and very awkward but it is the best way to meet people! Get plugged into a local church ASAP. Also, try to find a ministry on campus to connect with – don't stress too hard about making the right decision. Go with the ministry that you click with the most. Stay on top of school work or it will overcome you! Have fun!! Let your ultimate trust be in Jesus and about what He says about you – no matter how your days go it will bring you peace and hope." University of Florida, Freshman

"I wish I had gotten involved in a small group. A lot of why I had a rough rough freshman year was that while I had friends, I did not feel like they shared all my same beliefs and ideals. I was so used to having friends that were rooted in Christ like me that when I came to college, I guess I just expected to find that more easily than I did. I do not think it is hard, I just did not put the effort like I should have to find a church home and a small group of like-minded people. I think it would have made all the difference in my freshmen year to have had that. I felt lonely and sad all the time but if I had been around people that were finding their joy in the Lord, I would have been better." University of Alabama, Sophomore

"If you want a Christ-centered community, you will most likely have to actively seek it out. It won't just fall into your lap. So if you're an introvert like me, you're going to have to step out of your comfort zone a little bit to try new things. But that's what life is about. Learning to take steps of faith and lean on God." Miami University of Ohio, Senior

let's chat

What are some characteristics of a good community and good friends?

In what types of community settings have you felt most at home?

What are some tangible things you can do to make those who are homesick feel more at home in college?

What are three things you can do to seek out a community that shares your values?

If you are doing the corresponding Bible study, head to page 111.

chapter 7

Speaking of Relationships...Let's Talk about Dating

Pastor Andy Stanley says, "Are YOU who the person you are looking for is looking for?"

That's a mouthful, but take a minute to read it a few times slowly. If you are looking for someone who respects you, is committed to his studies and future, will go to church with you, will be a trusted sounding board and cheerleader for your dreams and goals... are you this person? Are you doing what this person would do? Are you going where this person will be? Do you find this person only at bars and then skipping class because they stayed up all night partying?

Think about the person you are looking for in a relationship. Write down characteristics that matter to you. I've included a few prompts to get you thinking in the LET'S CHAT section on the following pages.

Jarrid Wilson, a pastor and blogger, cites 23 qualities of a guy worth marrying (or in your case, dating), that might serve as a good start to your list. He loves God, he is driven, goal oriented, chivalrous, supportive, honest, he respects his parents, he respects your/his purity, he shows patience, he puts God first, he is reliable, he is trustworthy, he is someone you are attracted to, he is always willing to help those in need, he will pray for you/with you, he manages his finances well, he has a good reputation, he is willing to work hard to provide, he doesn't make hasty decisions, he is an asset not a liability, he has good manners, he is willing to protect you, he is always thinking on the bright side.

Your list is not to create your perfect boyfriend (no one will ever be that!), but to see in writing the things that you value most. Because what so many girls do is settle for less. They settle for being treated poorly or doing things they never wanted to do because they are lonely or desperate to be in a relationship. They convince themselves there is no one better out there. Sweet sister, don't settle! You deserve better.

Remember that a boyfriend will complement you, not complete you. When you seek fulfillment and completion in a partner, you will only be let down. Only Jesus can complete you.

As you begin stepping out and dating, if you find yourself in a relationship questioning things, then take a step back. It is likely the Spirit stirring in you the need to put on the brakes. And I know it is HARD. It is tempting to focus on the good moments and shove aside the times of discouragement, disappointment and dishonoring. Always remember you deserve to be treated with respect and kindness. Always.

Be prepared and remember the boundaries you have set. Stick to your tribe and hold each other accountable. Despite what culture wants you to think about "everyone hooking up and having sex," you are not alone!

No matter how cute he is or how great he seems, if he won't respect your decisions about sex then he won't respect your opinions on other things that are important to you. It will only be a matter of time before that comes out. He just isn't worth it. You deserve better. Trust God and the prompting of the Holy Spirit in you. You are deeply loved and valued by God. You are created in His image. You are worth being treated like a daughter of the King.

And hear this: whether single or in a relationship, God has a plan for you in this season. Sometimes we need seasons of singleness and more alone time to grow in ways God is planning to use in us at a later time. There is so much you can do single that you can't do as a couple. Embrace, rather than lament, this time. Take time to learn who you are, what you want, and what God wants from you. Don't ever think that any season doesn't have a purpose, characteristics to be developed, and lessons to be learned.

There is so much more suffering in being in an unhealthy relationship than not being in a relationship at all.

Don't settle for less, sweet sister. You have immeasurable value, and God has good plans for you. This life is hard and messy enough without bringing something toxic into it. Seek a partner that makes your journey more beautiful and God-honoring. I'm praying right now for Godly men in the lives of all you girls reading this today.

advice
from your older sisters

"I found a lot of shakiness I was unaware of because I was so supported in my faith at my Christian high school. I also was absolutely shocked by how much pressure there is to have sex. We had a relationship panel as part of our orientation, and half the students were part of a hookup culture, and all the others had sex during their college relationships. It became pretty clear that very few people would be willing to wait until marriage through a relationship." Olin College of Engineering, Sophomore

"I felt I had nothing rock solid to find my identity in and so I bounced around between academics, friendships, relationships, appearances, perception…stuff that is satisfying for a moment but never lasts / ALWAYS disappoints. I didn't anticipate the struggle and wanted a quick fix to make the uneasiness go away…during college, a steady relationship with a hot guy was touted as the solution to my longing feeling. It wasn't!!" University of Alabama, recent grad

"I was caught off guard by how much sexual immorality was so SO expected." University of North Florida, Sophomore

"I wish I had someone tell me that getting into a relationship during my first semester would be a HUGE mistake for me." Valor Christian College, Sophomore

"I wish someone had told me that romantic relationships are not a priority while in college." Cumberland University, Junior

"Focus your first year of college on making stable friendships – less dating, more connecting." Biola University, Sophomore

"Don't seek a dating relationship right off the bat. After just a few months in college, you will have grown so much…and a few months later you will have grown even more!" Grand Valley State University, Sophomore

"I wish someone had been REAL and RAW and STRAIGHT UP with me. I was in no way prepared for what was coming. I had never really been in a situation where I had to learn to stand up for what was right, so when that situation did come I was so overwhelmed. I also wish I knew that if you do make a mistake it's not the end game or too late. The truth is the parties were fun, boys were cute, the flattery was nice, but the emptiness was real and sometimes it takes a lot of mistakes to get to that point."
University of North Carolina at Charlotte, Sophomore

For more advice on relationships from your older college sisters, check out the **DELIGHT MINISTIRES** app and shop for the **FOR THE GIRL: STORIES ON DATING AND RELATIONSHIPS** study. It is a devotional book on dating & relationships in college. Topics featured include:

- For the girl who is anxious about being single
- For the girl who is ready to be married
- For the girl who has lost hope in love
- For the girl who is dating a non-believer
- For the girl who is in a new relationship
- For the girl who has dealt with sexual sin
- For the girl who is doubting her relationship
- For the girl who likes someone who doesn't like her back
- For the girl who is in a long-distance relationship
- For the girl who has had her heart broken

It is better to be by yourself for the right reasons than with someone for the wrong reasons.

let's chat

What are some reasons you or your friends have stayed in unhealthy relationships?

What does a healthy relationship look like?

What are you looking for in a guy you would date? What are some non-negotiables? Think about character, values, how they spend their time, how they treat you and others, etc.

Below are a few prompts to start your thinking. Write down what you value in someone you would want to date. Remember these things and keep them close to your heart. Don't settle for less on those non-negotiables, even if he is super cute, popular, hilarious, but also happens to be selfish, disrespectful, and always tries to talk you into crossing lines you never intended to cross. Remember what you value. You are worth it!

How he treats friends:

_____
_____

How he treats me:

_____
_____

How he spends his time:

_____
_____
_____

His values / what is important to him:

_____
_____
_____

His character:

_____
_____
_____

His goals (short term and long term):

_____
_____
_____

Does he love the Lord? Does he encourage you? Respect you? Cheer you on in your dreams? Is he reliable? Does he build you up and never tear you down? Does he give you space to achieve your goals and develop godly friendships? Does he strengthen your relationship with God, rather than drag you into tempting situations that compromise your values?

If you are doing the corresponding Bible study, head to page 115.

chapter 8

Loving and Serving Others

Love God; love others. It's that simple...and that hard! Look around... there is a lot of division and disunity in the world today. Some people will be difficult and hard to love. You have the potential to not only bridge gaps, but to shine light in this often dark and divided world.

God desires you to live in peace with those around you and to love your neighbors as yourself. This includes your roommate! Who you live with is a great place to start learning to serve others well. Instead of falling prey to gossip, complaining, and grumbling, practice the way of Jesus. Show grace, forgive easily, serve, love without expecting anything in return. The truth is, even those wildly different than you can teach you a lot.

Serving others not only glorifies God, but it also keeps you unselfishly grounded and is the best way to love your neighbors. It will foster humility and focus your eyes on God and others, instead of internally. It is easy to fall into the trap of thinking everything is about us and revolves around us. But this is dangerous thinking and a great trick the devil likes to use to spiral us into discontentment. Pride, entitlement, and arrogance are the root of much harm, both to ourselves and to those around us. Loving and serving others is the antidote.

You can glorify God with your time, gifts, and even your finances. College is likely your first time being thrust into doing life on your own. It is the perfect time to start practicing living within your means; not falling prey to the burden of debt and freeing yourself up to live life well and step into opportunities.

Practice giving...and if you don't have financial resources at this time in your life, you do have your personal time and areas in which you are passionate and gifted. Get in the habit of giving abundantly.

When you are faithful and a good steward of the small things, God will expand your territory to serve in even bigger ways.

Besides, serving others is an incredible way to grow into your calling and hone your gifts...

Do you love photography? Offer to take pictures at a local non-profit event. Are you pre-med? Volunteer at a clinic. Are you majoring in marketing? Offer to help a non-profit with a fundraiser. Are you a natural leader? Organize an event to raise money for a cause you love. Do you have a gift of teaching? Lead a Bible study in your dorm. Are you a great writer? Offer to write a guest blog post for a ministry. Do you have an eye for design? Create a shirt and donate the profits to a mission group. Are you a social media pro? Look into being an ambassador or affiliate for a company that donates a portion of their profits to a charity (and bonus, they will often pay you a percentage of each sale that comes from you).

You get the point...there is so much you can do even now to not only refine your skills and experience but also support a worthy cause you love.

There is no better time to start serving than now! Who knows, you may discover a passion and calling you never knew was in you.

On my website, I've included a link to some organizations that offer ambassador or affiliate programs where you can share their products (that also support missions/ministries) and earn a percentage on each sale. Win-win! Visit www.givingsquared.com/TurnNorth

Be somebody who makes everybody feel like a somebody.

advice
from your older sisters

"Pray to find ways to serve your roommates – service is the best and fastest way to grow close with people." Brigham Young University, Sophomore

"It can be intimidating, but you would be surprised how much can come out of unapologetically being a light for Jesus! You have no idea the impact you will make by sharing your faith / living a lifestyle that represents your faith will make on someone. God placed you where you are for a reason. Someone needs that light that only you have." Grand Canyon University, Sophomore

"Be kind to all you meet because, as you'll soon find out, college life can be tough. You never know when you can be an encouragement or shine a light for Christ in someone's life! " Arkansas State University, Junior

"Be a light toward others, even when you think nobody cares. I wasn't a Christian when I started going to college. The girl who led me to Christ was well liked but nobody cared to hear about Christianity. Except me 😊 Never let yourself get discouraged." San Jacinto, Sophomore

"Love others, even when it's hard and even when it seems they don't deserve it. You never know what they have going on, so let God be the judge and just love them like crazy." Furman University, Senior

"Pastor Levi Lusko preached at Passion Conference 2016, and one of the main things that stuck out to me was that there are two sides to every chain. He was referring to when Paul was in jail and chained to the Roman guards. Rather than thinking, 'I'm chained to these guards,' Paul chose to have the mindset of 'These guards are chained to me,' and he used his situation as a witnessing opportunity. I've had a lot of roommate problems throughout college, and this really helped me to get some perspective on how to deal with those issues." College of Charleston, Senior

let's chat

What do you generally do when you don't get along with someone? What if your roommate is difficult to live with? How can you show grace and love and even serve them instead of grumbling, gossiping, and arguing?

Look back over your "Calling" responses from chapter 4. What skills can be used to support a great cause or serve others?

Where were the areas your heart breaks for? What causes are you passionate about? Research non-profits addressing these areas and reach out to them about serving in some way.

What are three possibilities to explore where you can use your passion and gifts to serve others?

If you are doing the corresponding Bible study, head to page 119.

chapter 9

Time Management & Time with God

You've taken the leap! You've jumped into all sorts of things to find community, passion, and new experiences. However, you went a little overboard and feel spread too thin. If you find yourself in this position, give yourself permission to quit things. Your time is valuable, and college is a great place to begin to instill practices that use your time well. Author Bob Goff, says he quits something every Thursday! Our tendency is to always add things without shedding others, and we find ourselves overwhelmed and burnt out.

It's okay to say "no." Businessman Warren Buffett says, "the difference between successful people and really successful people is that really successful people say 'no' to almost everything." His point is we can't do everything well. And when we try to do too much, we end up exhausted, overwhelmed and doing a fair (at best) job at most of the things we are attempting.

Yes, you want to be a woman who keeps her word and commitments, but there will be many times where you can, and should, just say, "no." Don't risk sacrificing the great for the good.

Equally depleting is the chase for perfection. Deep down we all know perfection is futile. You will never be perfect...but Jesus is perfect for you. Don't be too hard on yourself. Give yourself grace. You are doing good work, sister!

If you find that sweet spot of passion, gifting, and need, perhaps it is an open door to walk into more deeply and shut some other doors along the way. Take time to see where things could go when you invest fully in them.

A repeated piece of advice from the college girls I surveyed was to get a great planner! Staying organized can go a long way to helping you stay sane with all of the assignments, projects, tests, and activities you will be juggling.

Speaking of being spread too thin, another recurring theme college girls expressed was not being able to find (or make) time for God with all of the demands of school (and let's face it, social activities).

What if you decided to give God your FIRST minutes each day? Before you check social media, send that text, get ready for class, attack that homework, study for that quiz. Kind of like tithing, but with your time. Giving God your first and best. That way even if you didn't get good quality Bible study time in, you will have started your day with God. And it isn't just checking another thing off your list; it is about building a relationship with Him.

Meeting God every morning will become such a blessing to you. It is a small, simple habit you can build into your routine. It will be your fuel for the rest of the day. Talk to Him. Thank Him. Ask Him to be with you during the day. Find a devotional you love or a Bible reading plan to follow. There are so many great devotionals that take under five minutes to read.

Jesus had the most important mission on earth, and He always took time to be with His Father in prayer. It is so critical...don't let it slide among the busy life of a college student!

A fully charged cell phone can perform countless functions. But without plugging it into a power source each day, it will slowly die down and before you know it the power is out...nothing is available. It has to recharge to do its thing. The same goes for you. Stay connected to your power SOURCE -- God. Abide in Him.

Trust me on this one. It will change your days. It will change your life. Even if only five minutes on those super hectic days. Make the time to plug in early and daily. Your soul will thank you!

I've included links to some great online and app devotionals to check out, as well as some beautiful planners on my website. Visit www.givingsquared.com/TurnNorth

advice
from your older sisters

"Planners make a huge difference! And make sure you make time for God. He will then give you time to finish all the rest." Utah Valley University, Junior

"I wish I knew that I didn't have to be involved with everything at first. It can be overwhelming how many clubs there are and what you want to get involved with, but you don't need to do everything, and simply, you can't do everything." Marian University, Freshman

"I wish I knew that it was ok to not always say yes to people, and that real friends would understand that I had to study, or rehearse for school." Bethany College, Senior

"It's okay to say no. It's actually healthy." Dyersburg State Community College, Freshman

"I wish I had known how hard college actually was…the classes, getting used to living life on my own, time management, and finding the time to spend with God." William Carey University, Junior

"Know the importance of a quiet time / being in the Word and finding your identity in Christ." The University of North Florida, Senior

"You don't have to go to everything. Don't feel bad if you don't show up to a club meeting every week!" Black Hills State University, Freshman

"The advice I would give is always hold on to God. Always try your best to keep a communication and relationship with him even if it's just reading a bible verse each day and praying every night and day." Sonoma State University, Freshman

"A lot is going to be thrown at you. There are SO many opportunities. Get involved but don't take on too much that you are getting burnt out." Grand Canyon University, Sophomore

"Don't overextend yourself. Give yourself grace to learn about your new surroundings, and don't try to immerse yourself into everything all at once." Bethany College, Senior

"Buy a planner and stick to it, you'll get really busy really fast. Continue to find God, and if you didn't do a lot to know Him before, now is your chance." Berry College, Junior

"Buy a planner and stay organized by writing in important dates, homework, and deadlines. When the stress is really heavy on you, it will become an absolute life saver!" Community College, Junior

"Don't be afraid to leave a group if God tells you to go. He will provide a safety network for you where he wants you to be." Texas State University, Junior

Here are a few **apps with devotionals or Bible studies** you can incorporate in your first minutes with God each morning:
- Jesus Calling
- She Reads Truth
- First5
- IF: Gathering
- Pocket Fuel Daily Devotional
- D365 Daily Devotionals

I also have a very short daily devotional that journeys through the entire Bible from Genesis to Revelation in a year. You can follow along at @jesus365.devo on Instagram.

Visit www.givingsquared.com/TurnNorth for additional devotional suggestions, as well as links to beautiful (and even affordable) planners.

let's chat

What is usually the first thing you do when you wake up each morning? How can you make time with God your new first thing?

How do you stay organized? Do you use a planner? What kinds of things usually throw you off track?

What is currently zapping your energy and your time? Is there anything on that list that you can quit today? What can come off your plate to make room for more important things?

How do you currently "recharge" with God? What do you do to stay connected to Him and His Word? Would you say you are usually fully charged with His power, or lacking? What can you do to stay charged?

If you are doing the corresponding Bible study, head to page 123.

"We won't be distracted by comparison
if we are captivated with purpose."
Bob Goff

Chapter 10

Technology – for Better or for Worse

Casually scrolling through social media, you are greeted with some of your high school besties. Perfectly filtered photos of big groups and even bigger smiles – parties, football games, sorority socials, new friends. Suddenly your upbeat mood fades to disappointment and envy.

Comparisons are hard in college when you try to live up to that girl on campus who looks like she has it all together, and often even harder when you scroll through the highlight reels of your high school friends' flourishing college lives on social media.

You are entering college in a time where everything is captured, posted, filtered, and captioned. Technology has some wonderful benefits and some devastating downsides. Be mindful of what you post and what you consume.

Studies on social media have shown that increased usage is correlated with sleep issues, anxiety, depression, envy, resentment, unhappiness, lack of substantive "real-life" relationships, isolation, and loneliness. A recent San Diego State University study found that teens who spent more time on smartphones and social media reported more mental health issues, whereas those who spent more time on non-screen activities like face-to-face interactions, sports, and religious services reported fewer.

Don't trade technology friends for real-life friends. Don't trade technology time for real life engagement. If following certain people leaves you feeling depressed or generates unhealthy comparison and competition, have the courage to hide or delete them. If you feel like technology is draining you of time and emotional energy, take a technology sabbatical. Delete that app from your phone for a week, or even a few days.

At the same time, technology isn't all bad. It can be used for incredible opportunities to grow and share your faith. Intentionally find Christian accounts that inspire you with short daily devotionals, inspirational verses, and women your age living a beautiful spirit-filled life.

And you know what else? YOU could be the one to provide that inspiration for someone. When you come across a verse in your quiet time or listen to a Christian podcast that inspires you, share it with others.

Consider starting a prayer or accountability group text. It could include friends at your school, friends from home, or a combination. It can be another space to pray and be prayed for. Recently a friend I haven't seen in years included me on a prayer group text. There are five of us girls living in different cities across the US. I am still so honored and blessed to be part of this group. Nothing makes my day more than seeing a group text pop up and then joining the others in praying for our friend in whatever circumstance she is going through.

Use technology as a tool not to replace real-life accountability groups, but to expand your circle. In this crazy world, we need all the support we can get.

Remain diligent and mindful about how you are using technology and how it is affecting you. Make a commitment to use social media to shine the light of Jesus, or to dump technology when it starts to drag you down.

I've included a link to some encouraging social media sites to follow on my website. Visit www.givingsquared.com/TurnNorth .

advice
from your older sisters

"I was caught off guard by how much comparing myself to other people was my vice. I constantly worried if I 'had everything together' or not." University of Southern Mississippi, Junior

"I was caught off guard by how hard the separation from home and missing everyday comforts that I had at home was. Even little things like my favorite restaurants. Also seeing my friends at other schools who looked like they were having a better time than me. Social media makes it look like everyone else is thriving." Appalachian State University, Sophomore

"I wish I knew the dangers of comparison." Dallas Baptist University, Senior

"Don't compare your experiences to other people's. It's hard to see others' new lives on social media that seem so perfect: they've joined a sorority or make tons of friends, but honestly odds are they feel as lonely as you." Berry College, Sophomore

"Social media isn't real, not every single other person is having the best time of their life – and it's okay if college isn't the best 4 years of your life because you'll hear that a lot." Temple University, Sophomore

Some favorite Instagram accounts to follow:

@soulscripts
@delightministries
@proverbs31ministries
@shereadstruth
@legitsadierob
@incourage
@girldefined
@my_darling_diary

@biblereasons
@morganharpernichols
@jordanleedooley
@livesalted
@givingsquared
@pocketfuel
@wellwateredwomen
@biblesandcoffee

@liveoriginal
@p31obs
@daughterofdelight
@kirbyisaboss
@godlyladytalk
@girlsavedbygrace
@inspiringhoney
@redeemedgirls

let's chat

Do you struggle with comparisons? How does social media impact this?

Take a look at your past few social media posts and the accounts you are following. Are they honoring God? Are they building others up?

Do you ever feel like social media is a time and emotional drain? When do you feel this the most intensely?

What can you do to eliminate the negative impacts of technology? Which category of accounts do you need to stop following?

What can you do to use technology to shine a light of hope and truth and God's goodness to those following you?

If you are doing the corresponding Bible study, head to page 127.

chapter 11

Take Care of Yourself, Be Grateful & Enjoy the Journey

Classes, grades, degrees, internships, resume-building opportunities...oh my! College is full of goal setting and goal chasing, but never forget to enjoy the journey. Don't just live for tomorrow. These are crazy busy, but crazy good, years. LIVE IN THEM. Take time to enjoy them.

Take time to be grateful. Gratitude even when – especially when – things are hard is a game changer. Did you know that Jesus gave thanks in the mess...BEFORE the miracles?

Countless studies have shown that practicing gratitude has so many positive life benefits. *Forbes Magazine* cited seven gratitude benefits based on various studies: grateful people sleep better, gratitude opens the door to more relationships, improves physical and psychological health, enhances empathy and reduces aggression, improves self-esteem, and increases mental strength. And a Harvard publication summarized a study showing that "those who wrote about gratitude were more optimistic and felt better about their lives."

So, sisters, let's do this! Start a gratitude list. Keep a physical journal, or jot things down in an ongoing note on your phone (and bonus, since you always have your phone with you, you can refer to it on those moments you really need to remember how much you are thankful for).

And don't forget the survival essentials along the way. Take Care of Your Health...Physical, Spiritual, and Mental.

Feed your soul well. Fill it with God's Word and God's truth. But don't forget to also feed your body well, get sleep, get fresh air, get exercise. Take care of yourself no matter how busy you feel. When you are fed spiritually, emotionally, and physically, you will be better equipped to handle all of the tasks on your hectic college girl to-do list.

Emily Wilson, a Senior at the College of Charleston, offered an important word of warning about the way college culture can sometimes encourage unhealthy self-care, "While self-care is very important, it's also important to recognize what is self-care and what is laziness. Yes, sometimes we need a day or evening to just do nothing, eat a pint of Ben & Jerry's, and watch Netflix. We need to be mindful about this, however, and be careful not to let it become a habit. 'Self-care' becomes a problem when you're using it as an excuse to be antisocial and procrastinate schoolwork. Society today is promoting the idea of putting yourself first and doing what makes YOU happy, when we should really be putting God first and listening for what He is telling us is best for us. Sometimes, proper self-care looks like spending some time with your Bible, then heading to the library to catch up on homework and eating some vegetables for dinner. We need to learn how to actually care for ourselves instead of using 'self-care' as an excuse to do whatever we want."

When you feel overwhelmed, afraid, or unsettled, go for a long walk, put on earbuds with a great podcast, sermon, or worship music...and just breathe, sweat it out, and talk to God. It is so therapeutic.

If you are ever feeling anxious or depressed, talk to someone. There is absolutely no shame in reaching out for help. Don't self-medicate with pills, alcohol or unhealthy behavior to fill the void. Instead, confide in a friend, mentor, or pastor. Reach out to your community – your church, small group, etc. – and ask for help. That is what community is for and you are not alone.

Many of the college girls surveyed suggested seeking out a solid Christian mentor...someone who has been where you are to process things with, hold you accountable, and offer support and guidance.

Feed your soul, mind, and body with healthy self-care; with things that make you stronger, energized, and fueled to be who God created you to be. Remember gratitude. And don't forget to enjoy the journey!

On my website, I've included a link to some great podcasts and playlists to check out, as well as links to some Christian counseling services if you are ever in need of someone to reach out to. Visit www.givingsquared.com/TurnNorth

advice
from your older sisters

"I was caught off guard by hardly having time to keep up with school, extracurriculars, work, family, and friends. Also not having a lot of time to take care of myself and my health." McKendree University, Freshman

"I wish that I had opened up to someone about the struggles I was dealing with." College of Charleston, Senior

"I wish I knew to go to therapy. There's nothing wrong with needing help and I wish I acknowledged my mental illness earlier than I did." East Stroudsburg University, Senior

"I wish I had been more open my freshman year to talking to someone about what I was going through because there is always someone willing to help." Grand Canyon University, Sophomore

"Eat right!! There's new foods and access to a lot of junk food. Take the time and money to buy healthy foods!" Marian University, Freshman

"I would've liked to know about how helpful counseling is and that it shouldn't be embarrassing." Texas State University, Junior

"Find a Christ-minded mentor on campus ASAP. Having an upperclassman or campus ministry staff pour into you makes all the difference." Boise State University, Sophomore

"Try to get enough sleep. Know your limits. Drink water. A lot of water." Union Bible College, Sophomore

"It's important to find your group of friends and remember to balance studying with having fun." Millersville University, Freshman

"I wish that I had a solid mentor." Bethel University, Freshman

"It's not a race on who can finish school the fastest. Don't have society pressure you to overwork yourself; know yourself as a student and what your limits are. The anxiety, burn out, and depression is not worth it. Take care of yourself." San Diego State University, Junior

"Make sure to take some time for yourself. You can't be 'on' all the time." OBU, Sophomore

"Don't be afraid to utilize the resources on campus – your advisor, your dean, counseling services, and more. They are there to help YOU be successful!" University of Northern Iowa, Sophomore

"Your mental health is important. College can be extremely stressful and can negatively affect you, so it has to become a priority. Be sure to take care of yourself and don't be afraid to seek help."

"Be yourself. College is a place where you get a fresh start to make new friends and learn new things. Don't be too focused on finishing fast, but focus on enjoying it." West Coast Baptist College, Junior

"Sleep and health are sometimes what you need to do. That alone glorifies God." Marian University, Freshman

"Have fun and enjoy life! Celebrate the big things and cherish the little ones!" Community College, Junior

Some favorite podcasts to check out:
- WHOA That's Good – Sadie Robertson
- That Sounds Fun – Annie F. Downs
- Proverbs 31 Ministries
- RISE – Rachael Hollis
- Journeywomen – Hunter Beless
- Going Scared – Jessica Honegger
- Happy Hour – Jamie Ivey
- SHE with Jordan Lee Dooley

Visit www.givingsquared.com/TurnNorth for additional podcast suggestions, Spotify playlists, and link to counseling services.

let's chat

Do you tend to get anxious or overwhelmed easily? What generally causes you the most anxiety? What tends to help you the most in these circumstances? What steps can you take toward your health when this happens?

Are you good about eating healthy? Getting good sleep? Getting fresh air and exercise? What improvements can you make?

Do you generally spend more time being grateful or wishing for something more or something different? In what ways do you think taking time to express gratitude changes your perspective?

What can you do to make sure you stop and enjoy the journey in the midst of the fast-paced college life?

What are three things you are thankful for right now?

If you are doing the corresponding Bible study, head to page 131.

Is what you are doing today
getting you closer
to where you want
to be tomorrow?

chapter 12

Rest & Reflection

If you get tired, learn to rest, not to quit.

I love this reminder because often we run ourselves so ragged we just want to QUIT. ALL. THE. THINGS. As I mentioned earlier, sometimes we do need to quit some things...but sometimes we just need some rest. It's in our DNA. It's how we were created. God modeled it and even commanded it. Girl, get some rest!

Outside of your regular quiet time, find an hour or two once a week to dedicate one-on-one Sabbath time with God; time to be still and listen, and also to get out of the crazy rat race for a moment to look at all the balls you are juggling from a different angle.

I know you may feel squeezed from all sides, but I promise this time with God will be an investment with valuable returns. Allow yourself room to get away, rest, and reflect on where you are and where you want to go. Without it, you may not even realize where you have gotten off track spiritually, mentally, physically, and academically.

Maybe you have even gone down a path you aren't proud of. God's mercies are new every day. There is no condemnation for those who belong to Christ. You have permission to ask forgiveness – to RECEIVE forgiveness – and move on with a clean slate. No matter what situation you find yourself in, God is there. He knows, and He loves you. All things can be redeemed and used for His glory.

So, whatever RECHARGES you, do it. A long walk, sitting by a lake or on a blanket at a park or in a cozy corner of a quiet coffee shop. Perhaps with a cup of coffee, worship music quietly playing, and journal in hand.

Take time to REST your soul with your Savior.

Take time to REFLECT on where you have been and where you want to go.

Take time to REMEMBER your passion and goals.

Take time to RE-ALIGN where things may be veering off course (in relationships, time with God, school work, your health).

Take time to RE-FOCUS on things that really matter.

Take time to REJOICE in victories, no matter how small.

Take time to RE-VISIT your vision...or create one!

Take time to RE-PRIORITIZE where yes's have slipped in that should have been no's...or vice versa.

Take time to RE-COMMIT to surrendering to God's will and to pursuing your calling.

Take time to REVIVE that flame that sometimes dims in the daily grind.

Meet with God and talk about these things with Him. Invite Him to guide you. He knows you better than anyone else. He loves you more than anyone else. He already sees the beautiful path He has laid out for you...take the time to let Him share it with you. Fear and anxiety slip away when you gain solid footing in God's plan. There is rest for your soul in time with your Savior.

I've created a worksheet with these prompts on my website at www.givingsquared.com/TurnNorth . Take it with you as you talk it out with God and journal where He is leading you. My prayer is this special time with God will recharge you and launch you on a renewed path full of hope, energy, and purpose.

advice
from your older sisters

"Learn to prioritize and not just for classes. Keep what is important to you at heart and put those things first, when you do not keep those things first you lose sight of who you are and what you value the most. I have learned to write down my goals and priorities in order to stay focused on the path I am chasing and it helps me to be able to pray about God's will for my life as well." Gardner Webb University, Sophomore

"It's never too late for something! If you want to join a club, sign up! If you want to change your major, study up on it! If you think you'd be more comfortable at another school, look into transferring! Be wise about your decisions and pray before making them – just know you have a choice." Wright State University, Senior

"I've always loved the metaphor of climbing up into God's lap like a small child. When you're little and you get tired or overwhelmed, or the world gets too scary, you can run to your parent and they'll scoop you up into their arms and hold you for a while. God is always there to wrap His arms around us and provide comfort, peace, and rest." College of Charleston, Senior

"Despite studying for school, don't forget to spend time in the word too!" Oregon State University, recent grad

"Never stray from yourself. Always know who you are and stay steadfast to the person you want to be. Even if you are working on yourself, do not be a representation of someone else. Find yourself." University of North Florida, Junior

"You need to make time for yourself. School and friends are important, but every so often you need to relax and be on your own for your own betterment." Marist College, Sophomore

let's chat

Do you take time to rest and reflect? Are there things you are already aware of in your life than need to be realigned or prioritized differently?

What recharges you? Where can you go to spend a good chunk of quality time with God?

What benefit do you see in stepping away and looking at everything from a 10,000-foot view, rather than smack in the middle of the details of the day to day activity?

As the book comes to a close, what are some of your key takeaways to equip you for a successful college experience?

If you are doing the corresponding Bible study, head to page 135.

closing thoughts

I pray you feel better equipped as you embark on this exciting new journey. When you find yourself struggling in certain areas, grab your book and reread those chapters.

Write down your prayers, and go back to look at them frequently. See where God has been there for you. Take the time to journal things you are thankful for. Make this a daily habit along with giving God your first minutes of each day. I promise it will change your perspective to one of more gratitude in all things and fill you with HIS power.

Enjoy the journey, sister!

Finally, I challenge you to remember these moments. And in a few years, take a step toward becoming a mentor to a new college girl. Take her through this book from the other side of the experience and show her the things God has personally taught you. Look back on your responses and notes and reflect on where God has taken you.

I'm praying for you. I'm rooting for you. I can't wait to see what God does through your life. And if you ever need prayer, I am one click away…just visit **www.givingsquared.com/prayer**. You can leave your contact information or make it anonymous. I promise to check regularly, and I WILL pray for you.

The following sections contain twelve short Bible studies corresponding to each chapter in the book, as well as additional resources to go deeper into some of the areas. I hope they will be a blessing to you.

And always remember to **TURN NORTH**. Keep your eyes fixed above, on Jesus. Seek Him first in all things. Allow Him to set your course.

With love and prayers,

Joani

resources

Resources and supplemental information on the different topical areas are included on the website at:

www.GivingSquared.com/TurnNorth

You'll find the following + more as I update it frequently:

- Links to encouraging podcasts, daily devotionals, books, Bible studies, social media accounts to follow, many recommended by current college students and recent grads
- Links to beautiful planners and prayer journals
- Links to Spotify playlists
- Links and suggestions for resources to reach out for help
- Downloadable Scripture – Who God Is & Who God says I Am
- Downloadable CALLING worksheets
- Downloadable REST & REFLECTION worksheets
- Downloadable ICE-BREAKER questions for small groups
- Links to information on serving and ambassador/affiliate programs to earn income while supporting missions/ministries
- Link to post your prayer requests

recap

Freedom, Intentionality & Boundary Lines
College brings about a whole new world of freedom. With this freedom comes exciting new territory and adventures, but also new temptations. Just because you CAN do something doesn't mean you SHOULD. Be intentional about setting your course and the path you are on. Discernment is critical and having boundary lines in place will go a long way to helping you stay on track.

But what about you? Who do YOU say that I am?
What you believe about God matters and impacts the decisions you make and the kind of life you will lead. College is a time to make your faith your own and flourish in your relationship with God. You might not have it all figured out, and that is OKAY! But it does matter what you believe. Do you believe God is who He says He is and can do what He says He can do?

Always remember WHO you are and WHOSE you are
Your identity is found in Christ alone. It isn't your grades, social circle, relationship status, failures, or achievements. It is Christ alone, and He has some pretty amazing things to say about who you are.

Exploring your calling
You are uniquely and wonderfully created by God, wired and equipped for purpose. The things you are good at, have gone through, and are passionate about are all part of your calling. You may not see it at the time, but even painful experiences can provide a training ground for the good work God has prepared in advance for you to step into. You are created on purpose for purpose.

The Battlefield
College campus is a battlefield, and the ultimate enemy is Satan. He wants to trip you up, get your eyes off Jesus and your hands off your calling. The devil is a masterful enemy and preparation is key. But, in the strength of the Lord and with the full armor of God, he's got nothing on you.

Homesick & Finding a new tribe
It is common to feel homesick in college, especially that first year. Everything is unfamiliar in this new phase of life. It's so important to step out of your comfort zone and find a tribe. But not just any tribe...one that shares your values, enjoys what you enjoy, holds you accountable, and has your back.

Speaking of relationships...let's talk about dating

It is important to think hard about the kind of person you want in a boyfriend. Don't settle for less. You are a daughter of God, and you deserve to be treated with love and respect. Are you hanging out where this type of person will be? Are you behaving in a manner that this type of person would notice?

Loving & Serving others

As a Christian, your charge is to not only love God but to love your neighbors. College is a great place to shine your light! You will have so many opportunities to serve others, starting with your roommates. Serving enables you to use your gifts and grow in your calling.

Time management & Time with God

Let's face it, college life can get overwhelming as you learn to juggle school, activities, and socializing. Time management is a critical new skill to develop. It's okay to say no – even healthy to do so many times. And above all, make time for God. When you seek God first, you will be better equipped for everything on your busy to-do list.

Technology – for better or for worse

You live in a captured, posted, filtered, and captioned life that is the reality today. Be aware of the negative impacts social media have on you – especially when it comes to comparisons. Step away if you need to. And remember that social media can also be used for good. It can provide a source of encouragement to you and from you.

Take care of yourself, be grateful, and enjoy the journey

In the chaos that can be college life, it is important to take care of yourself in a healthy way. Get sleep, get exercise and fresh air, spend time with God. Don't be afraid to get help when it feels like too much. Take time for gratitude. And enjoy the journey!

Rest & Reflection

Rest and Sabbath time with God are critical. Intentionally set time aside to examine things from a new angle and in conversation with God. Rest, reflect on where things are, remember your goals, re-align where priorities have gotten out of whack, rejoice in the good, re-commit to your time with God.

TURN *north*

A Jesus Girl's Guide to College
Bible Study

let's head north

The following pages contain short Bible studies corresponding to each of the chapters in your book.

1. Freedom, Intentionality & Boundary Lines	91
2. But What About You? Who Do You Say I Am?	95
3. Always Remember Who You Are & Whose You Are	99
4. Exploring Your Calling	103
5. The Battlefield	107
6. Homesick & Finding A New Tribe	111
7. Speaking of Relationships…Let's Talk About Dating	115
8. Loving and Serving Others	119
9. Time Management & Time with God	123
10. Technology…For Better or Worse	127
11. Take Care of Yourself, Be Grateful & Enjoy the Journey	131
12. Rest & Reflection	135

chapter 1
Bible study

Freedom, Intentionality & Boundary Lines

In this chapter, we talked about the new freedom you are given in college. With this freedom comes exciting new territory and adventures, but also new temptations. Just because you CAN do something doesn't mean you SHOULD. Be intentional about setting your course and the path you are on. Discernment is critical and having a plan will go a long way to helping you stay on track. It's important to establish boundary lines before your feet even get close to them.

let's head north

Let's look at how Daniel from the Bible drew his boundary lines. Like you, he was thrust into an entirely new environment. New cultural norms, new temptations, new expectations. He and many other Jewish boys about your age were moved from their homeland of Jerusalem to the bustling, but corrupt, city of Babylon after the Babylonians invaded and destroyed their homes. The king has big plans for these strong, fit, intelligent boys. He is eager to butter them up and have them fit into their new surroundings. He gives them the decadent food and wine from the palace. He **submerges them in the culture, values, language, and literature of their new home** for three years. He even changes their names in an **effort to change their entire identity**. (Reference Daniel 1:1-7)

What similarities do you see to college life? What cultural norms might you be submerged in?

"But Daniel **resolved that he would not defile himself** with the king's food, or with the wine that he drank. Therefore he asked the chief of the eunuchs to allow him not to defile himself." (Daniel 1:8)

Why do you think it was important to draw this first boundary line?

How hard do you think it was, given they were basically prisoners from a conquered land?

What do you think drawing this line will help prepare Daniel for?

Read what happened to Daniel and his three friends who requested alternative food in Daniel 1:9-21.

God blessed their faithfulness.

Fast forward many years, and there is a new king on the throne. Daniel also finds favor with this king as God worked through Daniel to interpret a dream for him. King Nebuchadnezzar makes an enormous image of gold and his eager officials make a proclamation that when the sound of any instrument or music is heard the people must fall down and worship the golden image set up by the king. The punishment for disobedience? Oh, just getting tossed into a burning fiery furnace. No biggie. Like little obedient sheep, at the sound of music all the people fall down and worship the golden idol. Well, not ALL people. Daniel and his friends refuse. **Another boundary line they won't cross. They refuse to worship anything except their God**.

Responding to the king, Daniel's three friends say, "If this be so, our God whom we serve is able to deliver us from the burning fiery furnace, and he will deliver us out of your hand, O king." (Daniel 3:17).

But they don't stop there, they further say, "But if not, be it known to you, O king, that we will not serve your gods or worship the golden image that you have set up." (Daniel 3:18).

Read what happens in Daniel 3:19-30.

Into the furnace they go, but God protects them. And not only are their lives spared, but the king worships God and issues a decree that no one speak against God.

Years later, under similar circumstances and a new king on the throne, Daniel both enters the lion's den and is rescued from the lion's den because of his **refusal to cross the boundary lines he established when it came to obeying and worshiping God alone**. (see Daniel chapter 6)

Through their obedience and unwavering commitment to the boundaries they established, **not only were Daniel and his friends not influenced** by their new culture and worshiping of false idols, **they were the influencer**. People around them took note of how they lived, trusted, and obeyed their God. And even in hostile territory, God is worshipped.

Think about the progression of Daniel and his friends' boundary lines...first, the simple abstaining from the king's food and wine, then bolder lines that would literally mean life or death.

How do you think drawing little lines early on will prepare you for drawing and sticking to bigger lines during more challenging times?

What kinds of things do you need to begin resisting while they are small and seemingly harmless before they explode into something extremely harmful to you and how God wants to use you? (with regard to friendships, actions, activities, invitations, etc.)

Jot down some initial thoughts on boundary lines you want to draw in college:

_____
_____
_____
_____
_____
_____
_____

Read 1 Corinthians 6:12 and underline it in your Bible - "All things are lawful for me, but not all things are helpful. All things are lawful for me, but I will not be dominated by anything."

Paul is talking here about the freedom we all have, but **just because we CAN do something doesn't mean we SHOULD.** However, this isn't generally the message we hear from the culture around us. The world shouts that we only live once, live and let live, enjoy your youth, eat drink and be merry, follow your heart, go with your gut, do what feels right.

What kinds of things do you see as technically "lawful," but not beneficial for you to do?

You will be presented with many things in college that seem permissible. Things that feel like everyone readily accepts are just "what you do" in college. How can this newly expanded freedom blur what is the best life for you to be living?

chapter 2
Bible study

But what about you? Who do YOU say that I am?

In this chapter, we talked about being grounded and rooted in who God is. College is a time to make your faith your own and flourish in your relationship with God. What you believe about God matters and impacts the decisions you will make and the kind of life you will lead. You might not have it all figured out, and that is OKAY! But it does matter what you believe. Do you believe God is who He says He is and can do what He says He can do?

let's head north

Read James 2:19 – "You believe that God is one; you do well. Even the demons believe—and shudder!"

James was the half-brother of Jesus. Before Jesus died and appeared to him after rising from the dead James knew who Jesus was. He grew up with Him. He played with Him and did chores with Him. **He believed Jesus was real, but he didn't believe IN Jesus – he didn't believe He was the Messiah and Son of God**. However, after Jesus' resurrection and Jesus appearing to him, **he believed IN Jesus, the Christ**. He became a leader in the early church to tell others about the salvation and redemption that comes from Jesus. So, James knows full well that you can believe things about God without believing IN GOD…without putting your faith and hope in God. In this passage, he is pointing out that even the demons believe things about God, but they choose evil and sin over Him and shudder in fear of Him.

.

How common do you think it is to believe things about God without believing IN God (that He is good, in control, saves us, and the one we want to surrender our life to)? How do a person's life and actions look different under both circumstances?

One day when Jesus was with His disciples, He asked them who people said He was. They responded with things like John the Baptist, Elijah, Jeremiah or another prophet. Jesus leans in and says, "**But who do YOU say that I am**?" These men were part of Jesus' team. He wanted to know who they say He is.

Peter chimes in, "You are the Christ, the Son of the living God." Jesus tells Peter this truth was revealed to him not from human knowledge, but by God.

The same goes for us. **God will reveal who He is to us**. It is more than an academic understanding. We can ask God to show us who He is! Jesus goes on to say, "….on this rock I will build my church and the gates of hell shall not prevail against it." In other words, **on this truth about WHO JESUS IS, the church will be built**. And this foundation is so strong and trustworthy that nothing – even the gates of hell – can defeat it. (Reference Matthew 16: 13-20)

Why do you think the foundation for the church is the declaration of WHO Jesus – God in the flesh – is?

So, Peter is probably feeling pretty good about himself. He was the first to acknowledge who Jesus was and even had Jesus tell him it was revealed to him by God. Good job, Peter!

Jesus then tells Peter and the others what will happen to Him…that He will suffer, be killed, and rise on the third day. Peter chimes in again, taking Jesus aside and rebuking Him (oh, Peter!), saying he will never let this happen to Jesus.

The same Peter who was just praised by Jesus is now being rebuked by Him..."Get behind me, Satan! You are a hindrance to me. For you are not setting your mind on the things of God, but on the things of man." (Reference Matthew 16:21-23)

Peter still had a lot of learning to do about who Jesus was and what He came to earth to do, but He believed He was the Son of God; the Messiah. And during Jesus' time on earth, Jesus consistently let Peter see more of who He is through personally witnessing miracles and seeing glimpses of His glory. Through all of Peter's mistakes and missteps, Jesus never gives up on him. He keeps Peter close in all of his glorious misunderstandings and continues to work in Peter's life.

On another occasion, Jesus is teaching the crowds that have been following Him to witness miracles and to hear Him speak. Jesus begins to say things that are difficult for people to hear and understand. So difficult that many of the disciples turn back and no longer follow Him. Jesus looks to Peter and the other disciples and asks, "**Do you want to go away as well**?"

Peter answers, "Lord, to whom shall we go? You have the words of eternal life, and we have believed, and have come to know, that you are the Holy One of God." (Reference John 6:22-71)

You see, Peter and the others didn't have all the answers. They didn't get everything about Jesus, and they thought some of His words were hard to understand, **but they believed He was sent by God; that He was God's Son and the Savior they have been waiting for**.

Peter and the other disciples weren't sure how it would all go down, but they believed in Jesus. **They believed Jesus was better than any other alternative.** The believed following Him would lead to life.

Does it give you comfort to know that you don't have to have it all figured out to believe?

Do you believe Jesus is better than any alternative, even if you don't have all the answers?

Let's rewind to the Old Testament. The Israelites are preparing to head north; to enter the promised land by way of Jericho after wandering in the desert 40 years. They send in spies to assess the situation. Here they meet Rahab, a prostitute and citizen of Jericho. She lives in the city wall...a city full of corruption and celebrated sinful living. **Rahab hears about this God of the Israelites and believes He is better.** She hides the spies to help them escape their mission unharmed. The Israelite spies reward her for her loyalty. They tell her to tie a scarlet cord from her window and when they return to invade and destroy the city, anyone in her house with the scarlet cord will be **spared from death.**

The scarlet cord in her window was a sign of her faith. Like the lamb's blood over the Israelites homes in Egypt when the angel of death passed over them and ultimately allowed them to be freed from their slavery, the blood red cord hanging from Rahab's window saved her and her family from the destruction that was to come to all of the homes in Jericho.

Rahab didn't have all the answers, but she wanted to be on "team God" even if it meant going against the comfortable and familiar culture around her. (Reference Joshua 2)

Rahab made a life-changing decision to turn from the false gods of her surroundings and follow the God of the Israelites – our God, the one true God – and live among them.

And do you want to know something else that is incredible? Rahab (the prostitute and non-Israelite) is mentioned in the genealogy of Jesus! She becomes the mother of Boaz, who marries Ruth, and their great grandson is King David. Ultimately Jesus is born out of this family line. (Reference Matthew 1:1-6)

How did Rahab's believing who God is change her life in ways she could never have imagined when she made that decision?

Believing in a big God doesn't mean you have all the answers or understand everything about Him. Rahab didn't. Peter didn't. But they believed. He was their foundation, and they trusted that though they didn't get it all yet, **He was who He says He is, and He is better**. They chose to put their faith in Him. They stayed close and kept learning. They chose to follow Him. And sister, He is so worth following.

chapter 3
Bible study

Always Remember WHO You Are and WHOSE You Are

In this chapter, we talked about the importance of claiming that your identity is found in Christ alone. It isn't your grades, your social circle, your relationship status, your failures, your achievements…it isn't other peoples' labels or opinions. It is Christ alone, and He has some pretty amazing things to say about who you are.

let's head north

One thing that is so clear as I read through the Gospels is the steady refrain that things aren't always what they seem. **The identity people place on themselves and others are often very far off of reality**.

The religious leaders of Jesus' day **have assigned themselves identities** of important, revered, knowledgeable, go-to for all things, assessor of others' sins, and judge of all righteousness. On one occasion as Jesus was passing through Jericho, he encounters a man named Zacchaeus. **Identities had also been attached to him**: small in stature, wealthy, tax collector, extortioner, sinner, unworthy of grace, despised. He scurries ahead of the crowd and climbs a tree for a mere chance to see Jesus as He passes by. Jesus notices him. Jesus stops under the branches of the tree, looks up, and calls him by name…

"Zacchaeus, come down immediately. I must stay at your house today," Jesus says.

The crowd grumbles. *How dare this teacher associate with such a disgraceful human being*, they mutter among themselves and aloud. But Zacchaeus is overjoyed. Yes, come to my house! Dinner it is!

We don't know what was said over that dinner, but we know that Zacchaeus' life was radically changed as a result of this encounter. He repaid an exponential measure of all that he had ever unfairly taken from others. His entire adult life Zacchaeus likely heard from the Jewish leaders that he was a sinner, that he needed to repent, that he needed to give to the poor. While all of this is technically true, their words had little impact on improving his life.

But Jesus looking up at him from the bottom of that tree, loving him at that moment, insisting He dine at his house, engaging with him…THIS forever changed his life. Zacchaeus was noticed and instead of being scoffed at; he was loved. (Reference Luke 19:1-10)

In Jesus' actions, He calls out Zacchaeus' true identity. He is a child of God worthy of love, grace, forgiveness. And it was this revelation in Zacchaeus' life that changed him.

May we not be fooled by false identities we give ourselves or let other people give us. Things aren't always what they seem indeed. **God alone gets to say who we are and no one is too far gone for Jesus to stop, look up, engage, and radically change**.

How did Zacchaeus' shift in identity realization impact how he lived? Why was it more effective than anything up to that point?

On another occasion, Jesus was invited to eat at a Pharisee's house. A woman enters with **an identity given to her** – and even spoken over her – by her community: woman of the city, sinner. **She believes Jesus is better. She believes Jesus can write a better story in her life**. She risks ridicule and rejection as she weeps at his feet, wiping them with her hair and anointing them with an expensive ointment.

The observing Pharisee tries to declare an identity for Jesus: fraud. But Jesus is secure in His identity. He doesn't even dispute it or try to clear His name. He knows who He is and whose He is. **His attention shifts back to the woman as He reveals her true identity: child of God; loved; forgiven; free**. (Reference Luke 7:36-50)

Are you secure in your identity? Do you feel the need to dispute and clear up false identities placed on you?

How can rooting your identity in who God says you are change your perspective and actions?

Back up again to the Old Testament and the story of Ruth and Naomi. Naomi finds herself in a foreign land. Her husband and two sons die. She is overcome with deep sorrow and loss. In her culture, Naomi had nothing. No heirs to carry on the family name (which was huge in their time). No one to take care of her. No family to comfort her. She decides to head back to her native land after years of being away. When Naomi arrives in Bethlehem, the whole town was stirred, and the women exclaimed, "Can this be Naomi?"

"Don't call me Naomi," she tells them. "**Call me Mara, because the Almighty has made my life very bitter**. I went away full, but the Lord has brought me back empty. Why call me Naomi? The Lord has afflicted me; the Almighty has brought misfortune upon me." (Reference Ruth chapter 1)

What is Naomi basing her identity on? How does this impact her actions?

Our sins, mistakes, misfortunes, and circumstances don't define us. Only God defines us, and He is always at work, even in the suffering and trials whether caused by our own actions, the actions of others, or even seemingly coming out of nowhere.

There is no promise that life will be easy or comfortable, **but we do have a promise that God will be with us**. A promise that He is good and He is working all things for His glory...the good, the bad, and the ugly. It is all in His hands. We are HIS.

Fast forward to the end of Naomi's story. Her daughter-in-law Ruth, who travelled with her, is now married and gives birth to a child. The women surrounding their friend, Naomi, cry out, "Praise be to the LORD, who this day has not left you without a guardian-redeemer. May he become famous throughout Israel! He will renew your life and sustain you in your old age. For your daughter-in-law, who loves you and who is better to you than seven sons, has given him birth." (Reference Ruth chapter 4)

God never left Naomi and Ruth. In fact, God had a bigger plan for their lives than they could have dreamed up. **Though their circumstances changed, their identity never changed. They were His**.

What circumstances in your life have you falsely allowed your identity to be based on? How did this impact your actions?

What can you do to remind yourself of your identity in Christ when facing tough seasons in life?

Look at Genesis 3:1 - One of the devil's favorite tricks is to plant seeds of doubt in us, whispering, "did God really say?" **Don't fall for the devil's lies or tricks. Stay rooted in who God says you are**.

God says, "You are enough. You are so enough. It is so unbelievable how enough you are...because I am enough...and you are MINE."

Jesus looked at the cross and then looks at you and says, "she's worth it."

Never forget your true identity, sweet sister!

chapter 4
Bible study

Exploring Your Calling

In this chapter, we talked about taking the time to explore your unique calling – the way God made you, wired you, and equipped you. You may not see it at the time, but even your painful experiences can provide a training ground for the good works God has prepared in advance for you to step into. You are created on purpose for purpose.

let's head north

One day a man named Saul was traveling to Damascus to persecute Jesus followers. But on the road, with zeal in his heart and execution orders in his hand, the incredible happens. A bright light from heaven shines around him. A loud voice says, "Saul, Saul, why are you persecuting me?" The resurrected Jesus Himself meets Saul on the road. Saul is temporarily blinded and instructed to enter the city. Meanwhile Ananias is told by God to go to Saul. God says, "Go, for he is a chosen instrument of mine to carry my name before the Gentiles and kings and the children of Israel." (Read Saul's conversion story in Acts 9:1-9).

This is the beginning of perhaps the most impactful ministry in the New Testament…that of Saul, also called Paul. Throughout Acts and through his letters to the early churches, many of which he planted, we see Paul as sold-out for Jesus. **He is so on point with purpose and calling, desiring nothing more than for everyone to know this Jesus he encountered**. This Jesus who saved him. This Jesus he loves and is willing to die for.

Take a look at how Paul describes himself in Philippians 3:5-6 before encountering Jesus, "circumcised on the eighth day, of the people of Israel, of the tribe of Benjamin, a Hebrew of Hebrews; as to the law, a Pharisee; as to zeal, a persecutor of the church; as to righteousness under the law, blameless."

Paul was highly educated, raised in a strict Jewish family. He went to all the festivals, kept all the laws, followed all the customs, memorized all the Scriptures. He was bold and zealous, willing to do what it took to carry out what he thought was right.

In what ways did Paul's past, upbringing, personality, and experiences prepare him for the calling God had for him?

How might your past, upbringing, personality, and experiences also be preparing you for your calling?

Let's back up to the Old Testament. If you've ever stepped foot in a Sunday school class, you probably know the story of Moses. He enters the scene at a time when the Israelites were living in Egypt. As God promised, they had become a large and prosperous nation. So much so that the Egyptian people began feeling threatened by them. As a result, the Egyptians oppressed them, forced them into slave labor and even demanded that all Israelite sons born be killed. But God had different plans for one of these Jewish boys. When Moses was born, instead of killing him as commanded, he was placed in a basket along the river. He was discovered and ultimately raised by Pharaoh's daughter. Slavery to royalty. **He grows up in Pharaoh's home.**

At one point when he is older, he becomes angry about the mistreatment of his Israelite people and kills an Egyptian in the process. This leads to him fleeing to Midian to escape punishment. He starts a new life, eventually marrying and having a child there. **For forty years Moses lives in the wilderness area of Midian.** (Reference Exodus 2:1-22)

Unbeknownst to him, the events in Moses' life are perfectly preparing him for the calling He will soon get from God. **He grew up in the house of Pharaoh (his first 40 years) but learned to live and thrive in the wilderness (his next 40 years)**. Two things that will soon come in handy. God is always working, even when we can't see it.

For the Israelites in Egypt, things are getting increasingly worse. **God hears the cries of His people**, and He has just the man to step in as His hands and feet. God appears to Moses in the burning bush in the wilderness, telling him that he is the one to lead His people out of Egypt. Moses is reluctant, claiming he isn't qualified and "slow of speech." But God insists that this is his calling, and He would be with Moses. You probably know the rest of the story. Under the leadership of Moses, God performs many miracles. **Moses leads his people out of slavery in Egypt and then through the wilderness for 40 years**... following God's direction, receiving commandments for how to live, and learning how to worship Him.

What unique experiences, passions, and circumstances led Moses to his calling from God?

Why do you think Moses resisted his call?

Look at Ephesians 2:10 – "For we are his workmanship, created in Christ Jesus for good works, which God prepared beforehand, that we should walk in them."

With the words, "Let there be…", God creates the world and declares, "It is good." With His hands, God creates man in His image and His likeness. With His breath, life flows through the first human body. And God declares, "It is VERY good." It is very good. You are very good. You are made in the image and likeness of God. **You are HIS WORKMANSHIP. You are created WITH purpose and FOR purpose**.

And in His infinite creativity, He has prepared in advance good works with YOUR NAME on them.

GOD HAS PREPARED these good works beforehand for you. The master creator isn't finished yet. He has a project He is inviting you to join Him in. He's been waiting for just this time; waiting for you. And it is good. So good...you have no idea. Your mind could never have dreamed this up.

As independently amazing as we might think we are, God is the creator. On our own, we just make a mess. We aren't different than those first humans who walked with God but still took the fruit. And just as it is BY GOD'S GRACE THROUGH FAITH ALONE that saves us, it is God who set in motion good works for us to do. The good works don't save us, instead BECAUSE God saved us and we said, "yes and amen!", we have been given the key to unlocking the good works prepared in advance for us.

Our job? To **WALK IN THEM**.

Why do you think God created us to have to choose to take steps and walk into the plans He prepared in advance for us?

The promised land was set apart for the Israelites, but they had to walk in. And just as the Israelites said, "I don't think so" initially, we often do the same concerning the incredible plans God has for us. "But God, it is too hard...I'm not qualified...did you see those giant obstacles?...I'm content enough right here; at least I know what to expect here...what if ____ happens?..."

Look around at the beauty, order, purpose of all creation. Designed in it all are some pretty incredible plans and purposes for you that have been prepared since the beginning...for such a time as this and such a person as you. Let's walk into them with confidence in, and power from, the master Creator.

Do you believe God has set apart good plans for YOU?

What keeps you from stepping into God's plans for you? What steps can you take to be more open to God's plans for you?

chapter 5
Bible study

The Battlefield

In this chapter, we talked about the intense battlefield you are stepping into on your college campus. And the ultimate enemy is Satan. He wants nothing more than to trip you up, get your eyes off Jesus and your hands off your calling. The devil is a masterful enemy and preparation is key. In the strength of the Lord and with the full armor of God, he's got nothing on you.

let's head north

Read Ephesians 6:14-18 with Paul's description of the armor of God available to us in spiritual battles – "Stand therefore, having fastened on the belt of truth, and having put on the breastplate of righteousness, and, as shoes for your feet, having put on the readiness given by the gospel of peace. In all circumstances take up the shield of faith, with which you can extinguish all the flaming darts of the evil one; and take the helmet of salvation, and the sword of the Spirit, which is the word of God, praying at all times in the Spirit, with all prayer and supplication. To that end, keep alert with all perseverance, making supplication for all the saints."

The belt of Truth. Know it. Cling to it. Strap it on tight. Everything falls off if this isn't in place. Steep yourself in God's Word.

The breastplate of righteousness. Your heart and soul protected – sealed and secured – by the blood of Jesus.

Shoes of the readiness given by the gospel of peace. A firm foundation in the Gospel. Planted and steady; ready for action.

A shield of faith able to extinguish all the flaming darts of the evil one. Get behind me, Satan. God is in control. I believe; do you believe?

A helmet of salvation. Your mind – the command center -- sealed and protected.

The sword of the Spirit. The Word of God, useful on offense and defense. Read it, memorize it, claim it!

With lips of prayer...at all times in the Spirit, with prayer and supplication.

And eyes wide open. Alert and prayerful with all perseverance for yourself and all believers.

THIS. This is how you fight the battles waging around you and in you. You have to be battle ready, friend. Fully covered in the armor of God. There is no other way to win this war.

Which piece of armor is easiest for you to grab and use in battle?

Which do you usually forget about?

Read Romans 12:2 – "Do not be conformed to this world, but be transformed by the renewal of your mind, that by testing you may discern what is the will of God, what is good and acceptable and perfect."

AND I LOVE the Message paraphrase… "**Don't become so well-adjusted to your culture that you fit into it without even thinking**. Instead, fix your attention on God. You'll be changed from the inside out. Readily recognize what he wants from you, and quickly respond to it. Unlike the culture around you, always dragging you down to its level of immaturity, God brings the best out of you, develops well-formed maturity in you."

Part of the battle is to keep from conforming to the things of the world that pull us away from the things of God.

What does conformity to the world look like?

What does renewing your mind look like?

Read Exodus 14:13-14 - And Moses said to the people, "Fear not, stand firm, and see the salvation of the LORD, which he will work for you today. For the Egyptians whom you see today, you shall never see again. **The LORD will fight for you, and you have only to be silent**."

This scene takes place after many miracles have led to the Pharaoh in Egypt letting the enslaved Israelites go. As the people begin to make their way out of Egypt, Pharaoh has a change of heart. He isn't going to let his free labor go without a fight. He mobilizes all of his impressive warfare and starts after the Israelites. Though the Israelites are finally free and have seen God's miraculous hand at work, they begin to cave. They assume a posture of defeat and actually wish to go back to abuse and slavery.

God tells the people to fear not. To stand firm. To see the salvation of the Lord. He continues, "The Lord will fight for you, and you have only to be silent." Some translations say, "**Be Still**."

Sister, this message is for you too. If you are walking in God's plans for you, **He will fight for you**. Renewing your mind is learning to fully trust and surrender to God. To have full faith and assurance that He is on your side and the ultimate war is already won.

Yes, there will be battles. Yes, you need to be prepared. But, at the end of the day, it is God who will fight for you. He loves you, and He has a plan for you. You need only to get battle-ready, steeped in His truth, His righteousness, and His strength.

How hard is it to be still and take things to God? Do you believe He will fight for you?

What does it look like in your life to be still before God and let Him fight for you?

How can all of these things help you on the battlefield that is college campus?

Chapter 6
Bible study

Homesick & Finding a New Tribe

In this chapter, we talked about how common it is to feel homesick in college, especially that first year. Everything is unfamiliar in this new phase of life. It's so important to step out of your comfort zone and find a new tribe. But not just any tribe...one that shares your values, enjoys what you enjoy, holds you accountable, and has your back.

let's head north

A group of friends hear the healer, Jesus, is in town. He's preaching at a house only a few miles away. The foursome pack up a few supplies for the trip and secure their beloved friend on his pallet, each with a corner of his bed resting on one shoulder. I wonder if they talked among themselves on the way there, or if they were unusually silent, keeping their thoughts to themselves.

They make good time, less than an hour. When they reach the house, it is packed. People even spilling out into the entrance.

They only let disappointment set in for an instant before coming up with a plan. They climb the rickety staircase leading to the roof, careful to balance their friend. Climbing a few steps and then waiting for the crew at the back to catch up until they reach the top.

They lay their friend down as they begin to piece by piece remove the roof tile. As the hole gets larger, they can't help but stop to peek in and hear what the teacher is saying.

Surely this is the one who can heal their friend. At last, the hole is big enough to fit the pallet through. They each take a wrap they brought and secure it to their designated corner of the bed. Slowly and steadily they lower the pallet. Though it wobbles, it lands in front of the teacher. It causes quite a stir. All eyes fixed on the helpless man in the messy bed.

The men rush down the back stairs and push their way through the crowd. Now the waiting. It is in the teacher's hands. What will he do? They are certain healing is coming.

To what lengths do we go to put our friends in the presence of Jesus? Oh, to have friends, and to be a friend, as these men. Not only do they have faith, but they are also willing to do the hard work to see it produce fruit. To not just say it and think about it, but to act on it. **We all need friends willing to carry us to Jesus**!

"Son, your sins are forgiven," Jesus says.

Wait, what?!?....they must be thinking. They came for healing, not forgiveness of sins.

Jesus always knows what we truly need. The heart of all of our hurt and suffering and most profound need is rooted in sin. It isn't that this man's health is correlated to his sin, it is that all of us have a sin issue that only Jesus can cleanse. He went there first because any other secondary need addressed will never bring peace and wholeness. And then Jesus healed his physical need, enabling him to walk out of the crowded room he moments before needed his friends to lower him into.

Where the world says, "you made your bed, now lie in it." Jesus says, "Rise! Take up your bed and walk."

Jesus says the same to us: "Your sins are forgiven….Rise!....take up your bed and walk." He stands ready to meet all of our needs, starting with the most pressing one of our sins. (Reference Luke 5:17-26)

Recap the lengths these friends went to in order to help their friend?

What was the result of these friends' efforts?

Do you have friends that would go through such lengths to help you heal and bring you to Jesus? Are you this kind of friend?

Read Ecclesiastes 4:9-12 – "Two are better than one, because they have a good reward for their toil. For if they fall, one will lift up his fellow. But woe to him who is alone when he falls and has not another to lift him up! Again, if two lie together, they keep warm, but how can one keep warm alone? And though a man might prevail against one who is alone, two will withstand him—**a threefold cord is not quickly broken**."

What does this passage say about friendship?

Read Proverbs 13:20 - "**Whoever walks with the wise becomes wise**, but the companion of fools will suffer harm."

What does this passage say about the type of company we keep?

Read 1 Peter 5:8 – "Be sober-minded; be watchful. Your adversary the devil prowls around like a roaring lion, seeking someone to devour."

My Pastor, Joby Martin, says, "One of the primary tools of the enemy is isolation." The devil is prowling looking for prey to devour. You need to get in the herd; find your tribe. Don't be alone in the open field as an easy target for the enemy. A healthy community surrounds one another and fights together against the schemes of the devil.

In what ways can our "herd" community help us in our fight against the devil?

Huddled in a room following His resurrection, the followers of Jesus wait for that which He promised. As often is the case, the spectacularly unexpected happens when the Holy Spirit arrives with sounds of rushing wind and tongues of fire. These believers would never be the same. They go from terrified to trailblazers; from frightened to fearless; from timid to tireless declarers of the good news.

Acts 2 gives us a picture of a beautiful tribe filled with the power of the Holy Spirit, as we get a peek into the life of the early church community.

Read Acts 2:42-47 – "And they **devoted** themselves to the **apostles' teaching** and the **fellowship**, to the **breaking of bread** and the **prayers**. And **awe** came upon every soul, and **many wonders and signs** were being done through the apostles. And all who believed were together and had all **things in common**. And they were selling their possessions and belongings and distributing the proceeds to all, as any had need. And day by day, **attending the temple together** and **breaking bread in their homes**, they received their food with **glad and generous** hearts, **praising God** and having **favor** with all the people. And the Lord **added to their number** day by day those who were being saved."

List some of the things this community is doing with one another.

What impact does this united, Spirit-filled community have on those around them?

Which of these characteristics would you love to see in your community at college?

Chapter 7
Bible study

Speaking of Relationships...Let's Talk about Dating

In this chapter, we talked about relationships and really thinking hard about the kind of person you want in a boyfriend. It is important not to settle for less. You are a daughter of God, and you deserve to be treated with love and respect. Are you hanging out where this type of person will be? Are you behaving in a manner that this type of person would notice?

let's head north

Read 2 Corinthians 6:14 – "**Do not be unequally yoked** with unbelievers. For what partnership has righteousness with lawlessness? Or what fellowship has light with darkness?"

A yoke is something put over two animals to enable them to pull together on a load when working in pairs. It is a tool to enable working side by side pulling the same plow to accomplish the same goal more effectively. But **where goals, purpose, or objectives vary, things don't go so well**. When pulling in opposite directions, you can't move forward or accomplish the task set before you. You are stalled, frustrated, and even pulled down the wrong path.

The people we draw closest to can help us go in the right direction more successfully or can send us woefully off track. The people we engage with, the things we do, see, read, watch, spend our time and money on...**do they complement our Christian faith or pull it in an opposing direction**?

Are we a light of positive influence where we are and who we are with, or are we stepping into places, people's lives, situations we aren't prepared for, and as a result, allowing our light to fade into the darker worldly things?

Some of the gray areas will be different for each of us, based on our weaknesses and temptations. What one can easily walk into, another would become unequally yoked with the worldly things taking over. None of us can serve two masters. God alone must be the Lord of our lives. If another causes a wedge of competition for our love, adoration, and submission we become unequally yoked.

What would an unequally yoked dating relationship look like?

What negative impacts might this type of relationship create in your life?

Read 1 Corinthians 6:18-20 – "**Flee from sexual immorality**. Every other sin a person commits is outside the body, but the sexually immoral person sins against his own body. Or do you not know that your body is a temple of the Holy Spirit within you, whom you have from God? You are not your own, for you were bought with a price. So glorify God in your body."

The Bible doesn't speak much of dating as the cultural norm at the time was marriage at a young age and often arranged by families. So, while the Bible doesn't necessarily provide a roadmap for dating as a Christian, it does make it clear that sex before marriage is not God-honoring.

Many of the college girls surveyed indicated that the pressures around dating and sex were some of the biggest challenges they encountered when starting college. Take note that the Bible tells us to FLEE from sexual immorality. Not take up armor, fight, or stand firm against, but to FLEE.

This is no joke, girls. **You are so valuable, and your body is a temple.** Don't ever let anyone – even someone you are close to and feel genuinely in love with at the moment – pressure you into sex. It is a union between a couple who have committed their lives to one another. So many women feel deep regret for having sex before they were married. Relationships they were sure would last forever crumbled, and they were left crushed, used, and brushed aside.

If you have already crossed this line, know that there is always redemption and restoration. A clean slate is available to you by the blood of Jesus. You can make a new declaration for how you live out future dating relationships. As you consider your boundary lines, I pray that fleeing sexual immorality is an important one you draw.

In his first letter to the Corinthians, Paul gives a **beautiful picture of what love is and what love isn't**. It is an excellent goal post for a solid, healthy relationship. (Reference 1 Corinthians 13:4-7)

Paul says **love is**:

- Patient
- Kind
- Rejoices in truth
- Bears all things
- Believes all things
- Hopes all things
- Endures all things

And conversely, Paul says **love is NOT**:

- Envious
- Boastful
- Arrogant
- Rude
- Insistent on its own way
- Irritable
- Resentful
- Joyful in wrongdoing

How can you apply this list to characteristics of the type of person you would date?

Think of examples of how each characteristic might play out in a strong and loving partnership vs. a toxic and harmful relationship.

Chapter 8
Bible study

Loving and Serving Others

In this chapter, we talked about our charge as Christians to not only love God but also our neighbors. College is a great place to shine your light! You will have so many opportunities to serve others, starting with your roommates. Serving enables you to use your gifts and grow in your calling.

let's head north

One day Jesus, standing at the temple entrance, observes the wealthy piling into the temple dropping large coins – lots of them – into the treasury. Each donation a loud clanging sound as it sinks into the trumpet-shaped metal receptacle designed to literally hear the size of the offering. Impressive nods abound as the clanging is louder and more prolonged. A poor widow comes and drops in two small mites, the value of a penny. They make barely as sound as they hit the collection vessel. **Small; unimpressive to the watching religious leaders. But not so to Jesus.** Jesus says her offering is more than all the others because she contributed out of her poverty where they contributed out of abundance. It isn't the size of the gift, it is the size of our heart. She gave everything. All she had to live on. (Reference Luke 21:1-4)

A.W. Tozer says, "Not by size is my gift judged, but by how much of me there is in it."

While this particular woman was giving financially in a sacrificial manner, the same goes for our non-financial gifts as well.

Maybe it's writing, creating, music, teaching, mentoring, leading, encouraging, tutoring, speaking, or any number of gifts. We are quick to be hard on ourselves; critical and insecure about what we have to offer. We think our offerings are merely a mite. Small, unimpressive, insignificant, of no use in the bigger scheme of things. But it's a lie. A lie that keeps us from putting ourselves in the game.

The woman had a heart focused on God and wanted to be part of the worship. She didn't make excuses… "I need it more than they do. It's all I have. It is so small. It won't make a difference. I'll give a little and hold back just in case."

We may be holding out because we don't think we have enough, or aren't ready yet, or don't feel qualified enough, or are afraid we will fail. We tightly cling to our gifts and passions, instead of giving them all away. **We think they are mite, but God can use them mightily.**

The truth is, God doesn't NEED us. He can make miracles happen with His words alone. He WANTS us. He wants us to step out in faith. He wants us to take what little we have, place it in the receptacle of our God-ordained spaces, and watch Him multiply it.

What mite (talents and gifts) are you clinging to, despite that ongoing nudge to give it to God? What is holding you back? What can you do this year to position yourself to share it?

Read Romans 12:17-18 – "Repay no one evil for evil, but give thought to do what is honorable in the sight of all. If possible, so far as it depends on you, live peaceably with all."

How can you, even in tough circumstances, strive to live peaceably with everyone, including your roommates?

On the night Jesus was betrayed to soon die a brutal death He was well aware was upon Him, He has a meal with His closest followers. He knows that while His time on earth in human form is coming to an end, these men will be the ones to take the baton and deliver His message. He not only wants to tell them how to live; He wants to SHOW them. He gets up from the table, grabs a basin of water and a towel and one by one He washes their feet. **A profound display of humble service and love**. An act He wants to leave them with as His time with them is coming to an end.

"When he had washed their feet and put on his outer garments and resumed his place, he said to them, 'Do you understand what I have done to you? You call me Teacher and Lord, and you are right, for so I am. If I then, your Lord and Teacher, have washed your feet, you also ought to wash one another's feet. For **I have given you an example**, that you also should do just as I have done to you.'" (John 13:12-15)

Jesus wasn't consumed with His current dire situation, His status as the Son of God, or the fact that He was doing something "beneath" Him. He was consumed with these men He loved, opening their eyes to what really matters; for them to see **how beautiful and essential serving others is.**

How can you metaphorically "wash the feet" of those in your circle of friends?

Do you typically jump in to serve or wait to be served? What generally causes you to wait to be served rather than serving?

Read John 13:34-35 – "A new commandment I give to you, **that you love one another**: just as I have loved you, you also are to love one another. **By this all people will know that you are my disciples**, if you have love for one another."

Following Jesus washing His disciples' feet as a display of servant love and as one of His last messages to them, He makes this statement. Of all the ways Jesus says people will know that we are His disciples, He says it will be **how we love and serve one another**.

Why do you think this is the most significant way to show you are on team Jesus?

Read Matthew 5:16 – " In the same way, **let your light shine before others**, so that they may see your good works and give glory to your Father who is in heaven."

Sweet friend, you can be a LIGHT in an often dark world. And when you choose to show your light and serve others and love well, **you point to God** – the source of all light. You give others a glimpse of who He is and why He is better than anything else they could be striving for and fighting for.

In what ways can you shine the light of Jesus in your dorm or apartment?

In what ways can you shine the light of Jesus on your campus?

In what ways can you shine the light of Jesus as you pursue your major and join organizations and volunteer during college?

chapter 9
Bible study

Time Management & Time with God

In this chapter, we talked about how overwhelming college can be as you learn to juggle school, activities, and socializing. Time management is a critical new skill to develop. It's okay to say no — even healthy to do so many times. And above all, make time for God. When you seek God first, you will be better equipped for everything on your busy to-do list.

let's head north

Jesus and His disciples stop to stay at the house of some friends, Martha and Mary. No doubt there would be quite a bit of preparation and work to accommodate the large group. **Martha gets to work...cooking, cleaning, preparing, possibly with an underlying desire to impress. Mary, on the other hand, sits at the feet of Jesus**. Open posture, heart, mind to hear all He has to say during this precious time in His presence.

Martha is distracted by the details and frustrated with her sister's lack of help. And it isn't that she doesn't realize how special this moment is. She was there when Jesus raised her brother, Lazarus, from the dead. She is keenly aware of the One in her home. **But instead of soaking it all in, she turns to Jesus and suggests He tell her sister to get up and help**!

"Martha, Martha, you are anxious and troubled about many things, but one thing is necessary, **Mary has chosen the good portion**, which will not be taken away from her," Jesus responds to Martha. (Reference Luke 10:38-42)

Yes, there is work to be done. Always. And yes, we must do that work. However, we must always **recognize what is most important. Time with Jesus is always a priority**. It fuels us and grounds us to do an even better job at the work we have in front of us. Time with Jesus reminds us of who He is and our true identity in Him. In the midst of the daily grind, it is easy to get off track. We need to continually plug into our power source.

Do you feel like you have your priorities in order when it comes to time with Jesus?

Are you typically more like Martha (busy and anxious about the details) or like Mary (reflective and quick to make time for Jesus)?

Read Matthew 6:33 - "But **seek first the kingdom of God** and his righteousness, and all these things will be added to you."

You are feeling overwhelmed...but seek first HIs kingdom.

You have all these ideas of things you want to run and do...but seek first His truth.

You are feeling tired...but seek first HIs righteousness.

You are in need...but seek first a supply of His word.

You are heartbroken...but seek first His comfort.

You have an important decision to make...but seek first HIs wisdom.

You don't feel like you are enough or have enough time, energy, resources...but seek first His power.

...and ALL these things will be added to you.

One of my favorite quotes from C.S. Lewis is, "**PUT FIRST THINGS FIRST** and we **GET** second things thrown in: put second things first & we lose both first and second things."

To me, it is a restatement of Matthew 6:33. Put God first, and all these things will be added to you. Alternatively, seek all these other things first, and you will have no time for God...and on top of that, you won't achieve those things...they will still be there. You lose both.

In the crazy busy life that is college, it is easy for God to take second place to things you will think you just HAVE to do first, and before you know it, you are left feeling like you aren't successful at anything. But when you make that time for God – when you SEEK HIM FIRST – you are better equipped and empowered to tackle the things in your calendar and on your lists.

When you are faced with a long to-do list or an important decision to make, who or what do you generally seek first?

How can seeking God first change how you approach and accomplish everything else?

Read John 15:5 - "I am the vine, you are the branches; **he who abides in Me and I in him, he bears much fruit**, for apart from Me you can do nothing."

What does Jesus say we can do apart from Him?

What does Jesus say will happen when we abide in Him?

What are tangible things you can do to abide in Him?

Sister, abide in HIM.
Start your day with HIM.
Seek HIM in all things first.
And the rest will be fueled with so much more power.

chapter 10
Bible study

Technology – for Better or for Worse

In this chapter, we talked about the captured, filtered, and captioned life that is a reality today. Be aware of the negative impacts social media can have on you – especially when it comes to comparisons. Step away if you need to. And remember that social media can also be used for good. It can provide a source of encouragement to you and from you.

let's head north

Read 1 Thessalonians 5:11 - "Therefore encourage one another and **build one another up,** just as you are doing."

Our culture generally fosters a scarcity mentality, where someone has to lose for another to win. It fuels an attitude that there is never enough. It tells us we must compete to stay on top; get our share. So we hoard things, knowledge, wisdom, lest someone else get more. We refuse to share. We are suspicious, resentful and afraid. We fear failure. Therefore, we often compare, think small, short-term, and afraid of change. We let the world tell us we should be jealous; that we should have what they have, leading many to tear down instead of build up.

But the truth is, there is abundance. There is more than enough to go around. More work to do, more opportunities, more need, more grace, more love, more hope.

While the world preaches scarcity, God's Kingdom preaches abundance. It shares possessions, knowledge, help. It collaborates, celebrates, and grows together. It embraces change and dreams BIG. Failure isn't as frightening because there are second chances. When we shift our thinking from scarcity to abundance, everyone wins. There truly is nothing more rewarding than to cheer others on and lift them up in their endeavors.

Do you generally default to an attitude of scarcity or abundance? How does this thinking influence your actions?

What has been your experience when you get in a comparison rut?

Have you ever genuinely cheered for a friend, even in a situation where you might have been prone to be jealous? Describe that experience and outcomes?

Would you say you spend more time comparing and feeling "less than" or encouraging others and building them up?

"Do not be anxious about ANYTHING..." Paul tells us in his letter to the Philippians. (Philippians 4:6)

How, Paul? I don't want to be anxious. What about this mess I am in? What about all the things I am behind on? What about this financial burden? What about all of this pressure I am feeling? What about my addicted friend who can't seem to pull it together? What about the balls I am dropping, the deadlines, the school work, the temptations? How, Paul...how can I get to a place where I am not anxious about ANYTHING?

"...in EVERYTHING by PRAYER and SUPPLICATION with THANKSGIVING let your requests be known to God."

Pray. Ask. Remember gratitude.

"And the PEACE OF GOD, which SURPASSES all understanding, will GUARD your HEARTS and your MINDS in Christ Jesus." Oh, how we need our hurting hearts, maxed out schedules, and over-thinking minds guarded by the prince of peace.

Paul closes this letter to the Philippians by saying that he has **learned to be content in whatever situation he finds himself in**. Whether brought low or abounding; whether in plenty or hunger; whether in abundance or need. He has learned the secret facing every circumstance: "**I can do all things through him who strengthens me**." (Philippians 4:13). He says God is willing and able to "supply every need according to His riches in glory in Christ Jesus." (Philippians 4:19).

Do you tend to feel anxious often? What do you generally do when you are feeling anxious?

Make a commitment to take it to God. Get in the Word, surround yourself with a positive and encouraging Christian community. And by all means, seek out professional help if you need it. There is absolutely no shame in seeking help. God is also in these details. He has equipped people to skillfully provide help to those in need.

Tucked in between the above passages in Philippians, Paul gives us this advice in Philippians 4:8...

Whatever is true,
Whatever is honorable,
Whatever is just,
Whatever is pure,
Whatever is lovely,
Whatever is commendable,
If there is any excellence,
If there is anything worthy of praise,
Think about these things.

Yes, there is hardship and suffering and evil and trials in this life. But there is also A LOT of GOOD. Philippians 4:8 is **a great filter to run your social media feeds through** (both what you follow and what you post).

There is no peace in comparison, dwelling on the difficult, or trying to solve it all on our own. But there is **peace that comes with focusing on the good**. Peace that comes from gratitude. Peace from asking God to help; to strengthen us and supply all of our needs.

Practice gratitude over comparison. Practice prayer. Practice dwelling on the true, honorable, just, pure, lovely, commendable, excellent and praiseworthy. It might mean turning off the news, taking a break from that group that tends to drag you into negative talk and gossip, or blocking a few social media feeds, but your hearts and minds will be guarded, making room for the overflowing peace of God.

Take a few minutes to scroll through social media. How many posts would pass through Paul's filter?

How do you think your mental health and attitude would be impacted if what you follow, see, watch, read, and do was filled only with these things Paul suggests focusing on?

What technology/social media habits or followers can you change today?

Chapter 11
Bible study

Take Care of Yourself, Be Grateful & Enjoy the Journey

In this chapter, we talked about how important it is in the chaos that can be college life to take care of yourself. Get sleep, eat well, get exercise and fresh air, spend time with God. Don't be afraid to get help when it feels like too much. Take time for gratitude. And enjoy the journey!

let's head north

Jesus and His disciples are faced with large crowds and little food. Jesus takes the little available – a few loaves of bread and two fish – and He feeds thousands with it. But **before the miracle Jesus gives thanks**. He takes the five loaves, gives thanks, and then distributes the food and even has leftovers. The gratitude preceded the miracle. (Reference John 6:1-15)

On another occasion, Jesus, along with weeping friends and relatives, is at the tomb of Lazarus. He has been dead in the tomb for days. All hope long gone. But Jesus knows that God has other plans. "Jesus lifted up his eyes and said, 'Father, I thank you that you have heard me.'" (John 11:41) You probably know how the story ends…Lazarus walks out of the tomb; he is raised from the dead. The gratitude preceded the miracle. (Reference John 11:1-44)

Even when things look impossible, we can give thanks. **Often gratitude precedes the miracle.**

How can you begin to give thanks for what is to come, rather than only what has already happened?

Read 1 Thessalonians 5:16-18 – "Rejoice always, pray without ceasing, **give thanks in all circumstances**; for this is the will of God in Christ Jesus for you."

Billy Graham says, "Nothing turns us into bitter, selfish, dissatisfied people more quickly than an ungrateful heart. And nothing will do more to restore contentment and the joy of our salvation than a true spirit of thankfulness."

Paul teaches us to give thanks in ALL circumstances. Not just when things are going our way. Not when we are free from any pain, suffering, or trials of life. In ALL circumstances. As Billy Graham points out, there is something therapeutic and mind-renewing about gratitude. It goes a long way to **re-shifting our focus and restoring our hope**.

Do you have a hard time expressing gratitude?

Think about the toughest thing you are going through now. How can you express gratitude even in that thing? Write it in your gratitude journal.

Read 1 Corinthians 9:24-27 – "Do you not know that in a race all the runners run, but only one receives the prize? **So run that you may obtain it.** Every athlete exercises self-control in all things. They do it to receive a perishable wreath, but we an imperishable. So I do not run aimlessly; I do not box as one beating the air. But I discipline my body and keep it under control, lest after preaching to others I myself should be disqualified."

What goals are you racing toward? How would you describe your life "race," both short term and long term?

What kinds of preparation and training is necessary for your race…think about the types of things you are practicing and learning, how you are nourishing your body and mind, who you look to as a trainer, who you train with, etc.?

What kind of additional things might you need to add to (or delete from) your training regimen?

How can you take time to enjoy and appreciate your "race"?

Read Joshua 4:6-7 - "...that this may be a sign among you. When your children ask in time to come, 'What do those stones mean to you?' then you shall tell them that the waters of the Jordan were cut off before the ark of the covenant of the LORD. When it passed over the Jordan, the waters of the Jordan were cut off. So these stones shall be to the people of Israel a **memorial forever**."

As the Israelites approach the Jordan River on their way to the promised land another miracle occurs. A flashback to forty years earlier when the generation before them escaped Egypt. The priests carrying the ark of the covenant walked to the foot of the Jordan River... and they kept walking...on dry land...through the river. The **waters were again parted to allow safe passage** of the Israelites into the land God promised them.

It is a miracle and a reminder...of God's past provisions and His continued presence.

God instructs them to take **twelves stones** (representing the twelve tribes of Israel) from the dry ground they crossed beneath the Jordan River and lay them down at the place they lodge for the night. The stones are to be a **forever memorial and reminder** so that **whenever their ancestors see the stones and ask about them, they can be told the story** of when God allowed them to walk on dry land through the Jordan. To **always remember** the mighty hand of the Lord.

The people also had the **first Passover Celebration** in the new land on the plains of Jericho. A **party of remembrance** to celebrate their ancestors being spared when the angel of death passed over in Egypt. They ate of the produce of the land. From this day forward, the manna that had rained down from heaven every day for 40 years, ceased. What a day full of gratitude, hope, expectation, and good food!

Like the stones from the bottom of the Jordan and the Passover ceremony, **creating a mark of remembrance is a powerful thing**. As time goes by we tend to forget even big things we are grateful for.

What are one or two tangible ways you can honor and create a remembrance of what God has done for you as you appreciate and enjoy your college journey?

How can this mark of remembrance be an encouragement to you when you face tough challenges in the future?

chapter 12
Bible study

Rest & Reflection

In this chapter, we talked about the importance of rest and Sabbath time with God. Intentionally set time aside to examine things from a new angle and in conversation with God. Rest, reflect on where things are, remember your goals, re-align where priorities have gotten out of whack, rejoice in the good, re-commit to your time with God.

let's head north

Read Genesis 2:2-3 – "And on the seventh day God finished his work that he had done, and he rested on the seventh day from all his work that he had done. So God blessed the seventh day and made it holy, because on it God rested from all his work that he had done in creation."

God creates everything in six days, and then on the seventh day of creation, God rested.

Have you ever thought much about this? Do you think God NEEDS to rest?

God rested because His creation was good. He wanted to take it all in. And while God doesn't need rest, **He modeled for us the importance of taking time to rest**...to soak life in; to worship Him at a slower and more deliberate pace.

The statistics are overwhelming about the number of kids, teens, and adults who are just plain stressed out. We are anxious and full of worry. We are killing ourselves by going non-stop and putting excessive pressure on ourselves.

Even at the beginning of everything being created, God knew this. He knew we needed to pause. He knew we were prone to burn out without rest and time with Him. He knew we wouldn't take the time to stop and look around and see the good among all of the stress and worry and work. He knows we need to rest and spend time with Him.

As part of the Ten Commandments, God would soon command Sabbath rest, but on this seventh day of creation, **He models it for us.**

What can you say about the importance of rest to God?

Why do you think we are so quick to brush off the Sabbath or even taking time to rest? Why do you think it is generally undervalued in our society?

What are the negative impacts of lack of rest?

From the desert God calls Moses to go back to Egypt and rescue his people – the Israelites – from the slavery they find themselves in. God speaks to Moses from a burning bush, and the first thing God tells Moses is, "Do not come near; **take your sandals off your feet, for the place on which you are standing is holy ground.**" (Exodus 3:5)

Around forty years later, God appears to Joshua (who takes command at the death of Moses) as the Israelites make their way at last into the promised land. Joshua sees a man ahead with his sword drawn. The man is described as "the commander of the Lord's army." Many commentators say this man was God the Son, a pre-incarnate appearance of Jesus Christ. The man says to Joshua, **"Take off your sandals from your feet, for the place where you are standing is holy."** (Joshua 5:15)

In both instances the place was holy. Reverence was expected. **God was in this place.**

When we approach God during our Sabbath rest time or even in our casual prayer time, we should do so with reverence. What if we too approached it as holy ground? What if we took our shoes off...a posture of reverence and not being in a hurry; prepared to stay a while; anticipating a holy assignment.

As we approach God and spend time with Him, we may realize our old metaphorical shoes don't quite fit anymore. There may be new ground we are called to walk on that require entirely different "shoes."

Do you generally approach God with reverence?

How can you metaphorically "take your sandals off" when you approach God in reverence and anticipation?

How about doing it right now...taking off your shoes, kneeling, hands open and extended...and surrendering to God. Telling Him that you want Him to be in charge of your college years; acknowledging that you need Him. Asking Him to lead you not into temptation and to deliver you from evil. Asking Him to reveal Himself to you and to give you discernment and wisdom when you face decisions and trials. Declaring that you are on "team Jesus!"

Have you ever heard the Toby Mac song, "Lose My Soul"? It's based on Matthew 6:26...

"For what will it profit a man if he gains the whole world and forfeits his soul? Or what shall a man give in return for his soul?"

Sister, the world is at your fingertips. You are on the cusp of immeasurable learning, growing, and life experience. It is beautiful and full of glorious opportunities. But always be mindful of the true prize...Jesus. **Never sacrifice worldly gains for your soul.**

My favorite part of this Toby Mac song are the words spoken at the very end. As you close this study, make these words your prayer to launch you into your new life adventure...

> Lord, forgive me
> when I get consumed
> by the things of this world
> that fight for my love
> and my passion.
> As my eyes are open wide
> and on You.
> grant me the privilege
> of Your worldview.
> And may Your kingdom be
> what wakes me up
> and lays me down.

journal

journal

acknowledgements

I would like to thank the following people who contributed to the book on the review team: Emily Wilson, Laura-Ashley Childress, Michelle Brezina, Meghan Kauffman, Maureen McGauran, and Sydney Greer. A special thank you to my daughter, Madison Ross, who encouraged and cheered me on throughout the writing process.

I would also like to thank the over 325 college girls and recent graduates who contributed to this study by providing feedback and advice on their college experience. Following are the schools represented:

Abilene Christian University	Fitchburg State University	North Carolina State University	University of Cincinnati
Adrian college	Flagler College	North Greenville University	University of Detroit Mercy
Allegheny College	Florida State University	Northeast Alabama Community College	University of Florida
Angelo State University	Franciscan University of Steubenville	Northern Arizona University	University of Georgia
Appalachian State University	Fresno State	Northern Illinois University	University of Hawaii at Manoa
Arkansas State University	Furman University	Northwest Arkansas community college	University of Houston
Auburn university	Gannon University	Northwestern University	University of Kansas
Austin Community college	Gardner Webb University	Nyack College	University of Kentucky
Baptist health college	Geneva College	Ohio State University	University of Louisiana at Monroe
Baylor University	Good Samaritan college of nursing	Oklahoma Baptist University	University of Maryland Eastern Shore
Bellarmine University	Grace College	Olin College of Engineering	University of Michigan
Belmont University	Grand Canyon University	Oregon State University	University of Minnesota
Berry College	Grand Valley State University	Palm Beach Atlantic University	University of Mississippi - Ole Miss
Bethany College	Gwinnett Technical College	Pensacola Christian College	University of Mobile
Bethel University	Harding University	Philadelphia College of Pharmacy	University of Montana
Bevill State Community College	Hawaii Pacific University	PMTS	University of Nebraska- Lincoln
Biola University	Hope College	Prairie State Community College	University of Nevada Las Vegas (UNLV)
Black Hills State University	Illinois State University	Purdue Univeristy	University of New Mexico
Boise State University	Iowa Central Community College	Red Deer College	University of North Carolina at Charlotte
Boston College	Iowa State University	Richmont	University of North Carolina at Greensboro
Brescia University	James Madison University	Rockingham community college	University of North Carolina at Wilmington
Bridgend College	Jefferson State Community College	Rose State College	University of North Florida
Brigham Young University	John Brown University	Rutgers University	University of Northern Iowa
Broward College	Kansas State University	Salisbury University	University of Oklahoma
BYU- idaho	Kennesaw State University	Samford University	University of South Alabama
Cal Lutheran	Lancaster Bible College	San Antonio College	University of South Carolina Upstate
Cal State Monterey Bay	Lee University	San Diego State University	University of South Carolina
California Baptist University	Liberty University	San Jacinto	University of South Carolina Aiken
California State University, Bakersfield	Longwood University	Santa Clara University	University of South Florida
California State University, Fullerton	Louisiana Delta Community College	Simpson college	University of Southern Mississippi
Calvin College	Louisiana State University (LSU)	Sonoma State University	University of Tennessee at Chattanooga
Campbell University	Lynchburg College	Southcentral Kentucky Community College	University of Tennessee, Knoxville
Carl Albert State College	Macomb Community College	Southeastern university	University of Texas Rio Grande Valley
Cedarville University	Makerere University	Southern Virginia University	University of Virginia
Centenary University	Marian University	Springfield College	University of Wisconsin Oshkosh
Central Michigan University	Marist College	St. Mary's College of Maryland	University of Wisconsin-Parkside
Christendom College	Mars Hill University	SUNY Cobleskill	University of Wisconsin-Whitewater
Clayton State University	Marshall University	SUNY Geneseo	University of Wyoming
Cleveland State University	McKendree University	Tacoma Community College	Utah State University
College at Southeastern	McNeese State University	Temple University	Utah Valley University
College of Charleston	Messiah College	Texas A&M	Valdosta State University
College of Saint Mary	Miami University of Ohio	Texas A&M International University	Valencia College
Colorado Christian university	Michigan State University	Texas State University	Valor Christian College
Colorado State University-Pueblo	Middle Tennessee State University	Texas Tech University	Vanguard
Cumberland University	Millersville University	Troy University	Wake Forest University
Daemen College	Mississippi Gulf Coast Community College	Umpqua Community College	Wayne State College
Dallas Baptist university	Mississippi State University	Union Bible College	West Coast Baptist College
Dyersburg state community college	Mohawk Valley Community College	University of Akron	West Texas A&M University
East Carolina University	Moody Bible Institute	University of Alabama	Westminster College
East Central University	Moravian College	University of Alabama at Birmingham	Wheaton College
East Stroudsburg University	Morgan state university	University of Arkansas	Whitworth University
East Tennessee State University	Mount Holyoke College	University of Central Arkansas	William Carey University
Eastern Kentucky University	Mount Vernon Nazarene University	University of Central Florida	Wilmington University
Elizabethtown College	Multnomah University	University of Central Missouri	Winona State University
Enterprise State Community College	Murray State University	University of Central Oklahoma	Wright State University

For additional resources or to order more TURN NORTH books, visit

www.givingsquared.com/TurnNorth

Made in the USA
Columbia, SC
30 December 2018